God's

Value System

Darren Twa

BlackStripes Publishing

GodsValueSystem.com

BlackStripes Publishing
19814 55th Avenue NE
Kenmore, WA 98028-3198

ISBN 978-0-9823574-0-8

For my children

that they may be blessed in their relationships
with God, family, and all people

Contents

Introduction

Do two walk together, unless they have agreed to meet?
–Amos 3:3

The Gospel is frequently misunderstood and falsely proclaimed. Even in the first century, the Apostle Paul constantly warned against those who attempted to draw people away from the Gospel toward forms of Christianity that included aspects of the Mosaic Law, Judaism or various forms of Greek religious philosophy. Over the ages, many in the Church have lost their focus on the Gospel by adding to it, corrupting it, refusing to live by it, or by substituting law for love.

Today the Church has fractures and divisions, with some contending that they alone possess the sole truth of God. I believe the Gospel is far more simple and clear than the "Christianity" surrounding it. The Church needs to regain a common focus on the Gospel, but first we need to be sure we understand the Gospel of the Kingdom. If we do, then other issues will naturally resolve. Our theology will make sense, our actions toward those in the Church will glorify God, and our actions toward those outside the Church will be redemptive.

A correct understanding of the Gospel will result in four benefits. First, it will bring unity to the Church. Second, the Church will concentrate on her mission. Third, it will allow us to correctly understand issues of faith and spirituality. And fourth, it will prevent apostasy.

The Gospel is relational; it is all about our relationship with God and with one another. It can be divisive between those who believe and those who do not, but God never intended for the Gospel to divide the Church. He intends for his Church to be united as his Kingdom, not separate kingdoms pursuing their own goals.

Our division demonstrates our lack of understanding the Gospel. Our lack of understanding the Gospel reveals how much we do not understand Jesus Christ. He calls us to enter his Kingdom by becoming like him. Since he accepts all those in his Kingdom, why is it so difficult for us to do the same? Perhaps we are not as like him as we think we are. Perhaps we need to have a closer look at the teachings of Jesus Christ.

As early as the second century, the Church sought to conclude which writings should be considered Scripture and which should not. This served two purposes. First, in some areas of the Roman Empire one could be killed for possessing Christian Scriptures. If someone threatened to kill you for owning a book, you certainly would want to know if it was worth dying over.

Second, purity of doctrine required determining which writings were acceptable for producing theology. Early Christian leaders knew the dangers of corrupt ideology and desired unity on the basic tenants of Christianity. We must continually guard to make sure the Gospel we proclaim is the Gospel left to us by Christ and his Apostles. To properly understand God's purpose for our lives, we need to clearly recognize the difference between the Gospel and our own interpretations and traditions.

Try to clarify your thinking by deciding what is most basic to Christianity. Which aspects of Christianity are worth dying over? What is Christianity in its simplest form? Which traditions and ideas would you agree are not part of the Gospel? When you answer these questions, you begin to see what unity in the Gospel should be.

Faith in the Gospel requires a readiness to die for it because the Gospel requires a willingness to die by its very definition. Jesus taught that being his disciple and becoming like him requires that we live a sacrificial life for others. Once we strip away all we have added to the Gospel, we are left with a love like God's. We are left with a love that offers to lay down our lives for others. Anything less than this is sub-Christian.

The Gospel of the Kingdom is very simple and is comprised of two parts: a part that we believe and a part that we do. Most simply, we believe that Jesus Christ died on the cross to restore us to relationship with God, and we subsequently practice that same sacrificial love for others.

As we seek to know the Gospel and God's value system that drives it, we need to be careful. Our perception of his value system may not really be his value system. To be sure that we are neither deceived nor ignorant of God's true value system, we need to examine the elements of it as revealed by Jesus Christ.

Overview

In Part 1 of this book, I will present some basic building blocks for understanding the Gospel. It begins with a correct approach to God. We must recognize that all theology is relational and has to do with relationship. This understanding will give us correct definitions for evaluating biblical truth. I will introduce concepts that will be developed more thoroughly in subsequent chapters.

In Part 2, I will discuss the Gospel of the Kingdom as Jesus taught it. We will see the important elements of relationship, value system, faith, and glorious transformation. I have sought to include every idea that Jesus presented as being part of the Gospel message. Jesus proclaimed the Gospel in terms of his Kingdom. He offered people the choice of recognizing him as King and entering it, or rejecting him and being left outside.

In Part 3, I will demonstrate what the Gospel is in its most basic form. Certain elements of Jesus and Paul's teaching are absolutely essential for people to believe in order to be Christians. Those elements are the Gospel, and only those who agree with them are part of God's Kingdom.

In Part 4, having clearly demonstrated the Gospel, I will present some examples and implications of how it should transform our lives. Action is an integral part of the Gospel, so we must not neglect that aspect of it. But we must also be careful never to mistake how we apply the Gospel to our lives for the actual Gospel itself.

Once we understand the Gospel, it becomes the basis for our discipleship and spiritual counseling. Through it we can evaluate our behavior compared to Christ and identify the areas of our lives that need to change. If the Gospel does not change our lives then we do not really know it.

Some ideas are so basic to the Gospel that they must be repeated to be absorbed into our thinking and understanding. By the time you finish this book, I hope that you can easily identify the priority of each of these ideas:

- All theology is relational.
- God's value system most looks like Jesus on the cross.
- Faith is believing the promises of God.
- We believe in a God who raises the dead.
- The Gospel is good news about God's Kingdom. It is a spiritual Kingdom, not an earthly kingdom.
- The Gospel is simple. There is a part that we believe and a part that we do. Everything else is tradition and interpretation.

As you read this book, you will certainly be exposed to ideas and interpretations that you have never heard before. Although you need not agree with all of them, I pray that you will not miss the essential message of this book: Center your attention on the Gospel of the Kingdom, be sure that you truly understand its significance, and put into practice the teachings of Christ.

Preventing apostasy

Modern Christians often require belief in too many doctrines. We erect barriers to fellowship and discipleship that God never intended. Rather than assessing one another by doctrines we believe indicate orthodoxy, we need to base our relationship with God and others on God's value system, and recognize the standard he uses for determining who is a part of the Body of Christ. We must grant freedom of belief on the many issues unrelated to the Gospel, and cease being critical of those who do not share our views.

If we fail to do this, we create an environment that encourages people to reject Christianity. By forcing our children and those who are interested in the Kingdom to believe ideas God does not require, such as our particular traditions and interpretations, we set them up to reject the faith based on a false understanding of God and Christianity. Once something non-essential to faith in Christ is undermined, if only in their thinking, it leads to disillusionment with God. Since God's value system as demonstrated at the cross can never be undermined, our faith must be centered on Christ's teaching about his Kingdom and his work in establishing it.

Part 1: The Gospel Is Relational

1 God's Value System

Knowing someone and having relationship with him is limited by knowing his value system, because only then do you truly know what motivates him and what guides the choices he makes. Until we identify all the values that dwell in a person's heart, we do not fully know that person. Even as we cannot discern the character of a man without intimate knowledge of his value system, we cannot rightfully know God apart from his value system.

Understanding who God is precedes any relationship we can have with him. To clearly comprehend what motivates God, we must understand what he values above all, and how he demonstrates those values. The essence of God's character and nature was most clearly revealed in Jesus Christ and most fully expressed at the cross of Christ. If we desire to truly know and have relationship with God, we must first understand his purposes at the cross.

Ethical systems

A value system is a system of ethics. Simply put, ethics are a philosophical system of determining right and wrong or good and evil. Ethics can be considered absolute in that they apply to everyone equally, or they can be considered to apply differently to individuals based on circumstance and on what each person considers good for himself.

Everyone has ethics. Some issues that you consider to be good are universally agreed on by people as good, such as taking care of one's own family. Yet other issues you believe to be good may be regarded by others as only your opinion. Even when we say a man has no ethics, he still has ethics; they are simply not ethics that match ours. When something is said to be unethical, it is a judgment based on the speaker's ethical system. We tend to measure the actions of others based on our own value systems rather than theirs.

Laws are value systems or codes of ethics that have been adopted as a common system of rules by which the inhabitants of a legal district must live. It is not true that morality cannot be legislated. Every law is an attempt to force others to live by a value system, which is a form of morality. However, the point of that statement is the heart cannot be transformed by external forces.

Ethical systems are guides that help us change to become like someone or something. Inner change is accomplished through changing a person's value system. When you choose an ethical system, you need to be sure about what you believe you are and what you think you should become. In other words, if you do not know what you want to be like, you will have trouble finding a value system that will guide you to any particular end.

The Christian can be sure of what he is to become. We are to become Christ-like. All ethics in Christianity must be measured by Christ. Any ethical system a Christian follows, or counseling he receives, must be guiding him to become like Christ. Transformation to Christ-likeness is the end goal for every believer, and only occurs by adopting his value system.

There is a value system better than every other value system. It can guide us in how we should live in relationship with one another, and it can provide solutions to all of mankind's problems. This value system is the value system of God as revealed in the Gospel of Jesus Christ.

The Gospel reveals God's value system

The center point of Christianity is Christ's death on the cross. Unless we understand the purpose of his death, we cannot clearly understand God. Knowing the Gospel gives us great insight into the character and nature of God because it reveals his value system. In order to love God and love others, we must know the Gospel without confusing it with various traditions and interpretations held by churches. If our idea of the Gospel is corrupt, discovering God's value system becomes much more difficult.

God's value system is sacrificial love for the benefit of others. Christ's death was a sacrifice that flowed from his love for us. Though very costly to him, he sacrificed that we might be changed by his loss. We benefit by receiving the mercy, grace and restored relationship that was unobtainable apart from his work on our behalf.

Love as a value system

One day a Pharisee asked Jesus what the greatest commandment was. Jesus answered that a person was to love the Lord God with all his being and to love his neighbor as he loves himself.[1] Thinking of God's value system as a set of rules governing actions, behavior, and styles of dress is a common mistake. Since love for God and others cannot be achieved through following a list of rules, we need to understand what it means to love one another in relationship. From what Jesus said, we can immediately learn two details about God's value system. First, it does not harm others; and, second, it seeks to help them.

There is a significant difference between what Jesus taught and what other teachers in his day taught. Hillel, a Pharisee, summed up the Law[2] this way: "That which is hateful to you do not do to your fellow man." But Jesus said, "Whatever you wish that others would do to you, do also to them, for this is the Law and the Prophets."[3]

Hillel's statement addressed the negative side of relationship while Jesus stressed the positive. Jesus does not allow us to ignore the needs of others. His disciples cannot merely refrain from doing evil—they are obliged to do good.

When we love someone, we put that other person's needs and desires before our own. We do not need a list mandating what we must do or not do to others. Simply thinking about how our actions affect others will guide us in how we should treat them. Loving actions help others, while sinful actions exploit them. Loving others allows us to live beyond merely following a set of rules.

---

1. Matthew 22:36-39 "Teacher, which is the great commandment in the Law?" And he said to him, "You shall love the Lord your God with all your heart and with all your soul and with all your mind. This is the great and first commandment. And a second is like it: You shall love your neighbor as yourself."

2. By "Law" I refer to the Law of Moses, or the Mosaic Law.

3. Matthew 7:12

We can often determine God's value system in various situations by examining the effect an action has on others. Many ethical issues and questions can be solved by simply answering the following question: *Does this action exploit another person or is it sacrificial love?* That one question will help us determine right and wrong, and good and evil.

Later, we will study the other teachings and actions of Jesus that conveyed his value system to his disciples. For now, consider all the aspects of God's character that are revealed by Jesus Christ dying on the cross:

- God has a moral system that we breached.
- God is just and needed to punish us because of that breach.
- God is loving by treating us in a way that we do not deserve.
- God is forgiving by not punishing us.
- God chose to take the punishment his justice demands.
- God desires relationship with us, and intends that we be reconciled to him by loving like he does.

These truths are found in the death of Christ on the cross. Of course, we have the Bible and the oral traditions of the Church that help us gain all that understanding. But the point is simple: meditation on the cross of Christ can vividly reveal God's value system.

God's value system is sacrificial love for the benefit of others. It is primarily relational, and it is how we are to live and treat one another. If we measure our lives by his kind of love rather than by our own ideas of what he desires, we will better understand God and more faithfully live as he intends.

Once we fully understand the Gospel and the work of Christ on the cross, we will have the means by which we can truly know the character and nature of God. Once we know God, relationship with him becomes based on who he truly is rather than any misunderstandings we might have of him.

2 Relationship and Value System

Using relationship as the basis for understanding God and our connection to him brings clarity to how and why we should live. Theological discussions usually follow two main approaches: biblical theology and systematic theology. Biblical theology attempts to understand the themes of the Bible, while systematic theology attempts to understand the nature of God, man, sin, and salvation by breaking down the areas of study into specific categories.

Discussing theology in terms of relationship can bring both of these approaches together. Once you understand the importance of relationship and value system, it will become apparent how all theology is centered on relationship: God exists in relationship, we were created for relationship, sin destroys relationship, death is the loss of relationship, and reconciliation is the restoration of relationship. Many more biblical themes can easily be expressed in terms of relationship. Once we understand biblical relationships, we will be able to see that the Bible contains the story of how God revealed himself to man by means of his value system.

Created for relationship

God created us as relational beings. This is one reason why loneliness is so painful, and why abandonment or betrayal wounds our hearts so deeply. But it is also why we find deep joy in loving one another. Because God created us to have relationship with him and others, relationship is a fundamental part of our purpose.

God is inherently relational. We believe in a triune God that exists as Father, Son, and Holy Spirit. We believe he is one, yet exists as three persons; he forever exists in perfect relationship. Perfect unity in relationship flows from perfect agreement in value system.

Modeled after God, we were created to have relationship with him, with each other, and with the rest of Creation. Relationship is the purpose of Creation. Although there are many aspects to our bearing God's image, creating relationship is a significant part of the image of God in us.

Creating relationships is being like God. The marriage relationship demonstrates this, for it is the creation of a new relationship. Being married is essentially relational. One aspect of marriage is procreation, which is the ultimate in creating new relationship.

We are most like God when we pursue relationships, whether creating, extending, or restoring them. Conversely, destroying relationship is unlike God; it is what the devil does. He comes to steal, kill, and destroy.

Value system is the basis for relationship

Before we further explore the elements of God's value system, we need to understand the effect value system has on relationship. Relationship is based on sharing a common value system. The quality of any relationship has as its foundation how much the two parties are alike in what they value.

No two people agree on everything, and no two people give equal weight to the things they value; but where there are common values and agreement on the weight each has as a motivation for living, there is a deep bond in the relationship. The depth and quality of the relationship depends on which values are held in common.

Obviously, the reverse is also true. If something is extremely important to you, whereas I have little regard for it, at that point our relationship will suffer. When there is significant disagreement on many or crucial issues, we say that we have little in common. The ability to develop a meaningful relationship with each other will be difficult, if not impossible.

Early in marriage, couples often have many conflicts as they begin to realize the differences in their value systems. These differences not only produce conflict; they reveal how different the other person is from what each had expected. Discovering who another person truly is revolves around learning his or her value system. Strong marriages require a discovery of the values motivating the other person, as well as agreement on sharing the most important ones.

All values, even non-moral ones, affect relationship. Christian parents and children may judge moral issues (such as lifestyles) as though they are not moral; or they may do the opposite and judge non-moral issues (such as hairstyles) as though they are moral. By doing this, they confuse culture with Christianity. Even if the disagreement is not over a moral issue, conflict in relationship occurs when people live by different value systems.

All conflict in relationship is conflict over value system. Relationships break down when people are unable or unwilling to agree on the value behind the conflict. In order to restore a broken relationship, the two parties must come to an agreement on values. True reconciliation only occurs when one or both people are willing to acknowledge the problem, and then seek to remove the differences between them.

Whenever you have conflict and difficulty in your relationships, it is because either you or the other person is not living according to God's value system. Do not immediately blame the other person, and do not assume you are the one who is right. Both of you might be wrong. Examine yourself to see if it is your own failure in living by God's value system that is producing the conflict.

Relational conflict with God

The measure and standard of love is God's sacrificial love for the benefit of others.[1] If we possess the exact same value system as God, then we know we have relationship with him. The way God expects us to express our love for him is by adopting his value system of love for others. Relationship with God and loving him is directly related to our loving one another.

We know how much we love God only by how much we love other

---

1. 1 John 4:10 In this is love, not that we have loved God but that he loved us and sent his Son to be the propitiation for our sins.

1 John 3:16-18 By this we know love, that he laid down his life for us, and we ought to lay down our lives for the brothers. But if anyone has the world's goods and sees his brother in need, yet closes his heart against him, how does God's love abide in him? Little children, let us not love in word or talk but in deed and in truth.

people; our love for God cannot be separated from how we treat others. The value system that we demonstrate to those around us is our true value system. We do not have one way of treating God and another way of treating people. If we do not love others, then we do not love God either.[2]

Our value systems may overlap God's to a degree, but we tend to act out of self-love much of the time. That self-love is at the expense of others and is displayed when we hurt them. When we mistreat others, we demonstrate how much we do not share God's values.

In order to have a good relationship with God, we must share his system of values. We must think the same as he does about what is good and evil, right and wrong, beautiful and ugly. The more similar our values are to God's, the closer our relationship with him becomes. Failure in our relationships with other people is often a sign that we have a relational conflict with God. Any time this occurs, we can be sure that God's value system is right and that ours needs changing.

Any differences between our value system and God's produce conflict in our relationship with him. To restore relationship with God, we must know and share his value system; and to do that, we must examine the cross. Jesus died on the cross to deal with our value systems.[3] Since all theology is relational, we must understand the relational reasons for why Christ died on the cross.

---

2. 1 John 3:9-10 No one born of God makes a practice of sinning, for God's seed abides in him, and he cannot keep on sinning because he has been born of God. By this it is evident who are the children of God, and who are the children of the devil: whoever does not practice righteousness is not of God, nor is the one who does not love his brother.

3. See Appendix: Justification, Sanctification, and Glorification

3 Sin Is a Relational Problem

You have probably heard many sermons on the subject of sin over the years. You have likely been taught that sin is part of the moral realm; that some actions are by their nature good and others are inherently evil. That concept needs refining.

There are many fine definitions of sin and clear Bible verses to support them. According to the Westminster Shorter Catechism, "Sin is any want of conformity unto, or transgression of, the law of God." Bible verses that seek to describe the nature of sin often do so in terms of law or according to predefined sets of rules.[1] Right is right and wrong is sin.[2] But this does not define sin as much as describe it.

To begin understanding sin, we need to ask some questions. Do you have a tendency to sin against someone who is unknown to you more than to those you know? Would you sin against a stranger more easily than a friend? Are you more likely to do good to a neighbor than to a Samaritan?[3] Do you more willingly sin when you have the perception that it does not hurt anyone? This perception may be real, imagined or self-delusional. That is why we continue to have "moral" polls that ask, "If you were guaranteed not to get caught, would you…?"

1. 1 John 3:4 Everyone who makes a practice of sinning also practices lawlessness; sin is lawlessness.

2. 1 John 5:17 All wrongdoing is sin, but there is sin that does not lead to death.

3. Luke 10:25-37

Sin always affects someone

Although many people think it is possible to sin in isolation, that they could do something sinful without it having an effect on anyone else, they are mistaken. It is not possible to sin without affecting another person because sin is always an offense *against* someone. Similarly, a transgression is an offense against a lawgiver; either against the person himself or the law he has given.

Since sin has to do with the moral law of God, the measure of sin is not a set of rules, but the Person of God. *Sin is when we are not like God.* Sin is when we desire what God does not and would not desire. We can determine whether or not something is sinful by comparing and contrasting it to the value system (the ethics or morals) of God.

Understanding sin requires more than listing *what* is wrong. Do not focus on the legal status of your actions; instead, learn to think about *why* something is wrong. It is wrong because it hurts someone, either God or another person. Sin always affects relationship and is by its very nature an offense against another person. Sin is primarily a relational issue.[4]

If sin is relational, why do you sin? Why would you break relationship, either with God or those you love? Sin reveals your value system. *Sin reveals what you value more than relationships.* James addressed a significant aspect of sin by pointing to the desires of our hearts, that which we want, as the source of sin.[5] We sin because of what we desire in opposition to the desires of others. These passions within us cause us to quarrel and fight with others.[6]

---

4. Understanding the relational aspect of sin helps distinguish between sin and accidents. Sin is an issue of value system—personal motivations and desires—and its consequences as it relates to others. When an accident occurs, we understand that it has nothing to do with value system. It is something that occurs apart from choice and values. However, an accident that happens while practicing a sinful value system is a different matter. For example, a person who injures another while driving drunk did not have an accident. The injury to the other was the direct result of a value system that permitted him to drive while impaired.

5. James 1:13-15 Let no one say when he is tempted, "I am being tempted by God," for God cannot be tempted with evil, and he himself tempts no one. But each person is tempted when he is lured and enticed by his own desire. Then desire when it has conceived gives birth to sin, and sin when it is fully grown brings forth death.

6. James 4:1-2 What causes quarrels and what causes fights among you? Is it not this, that your passions are at war within you? You desire and do not have, so you murder. You covet and cannot obtain, so you fight and quarrel.

Our relationships fail because we desire to please ourselves more than we desire good relationships with others. Think about a relationship problem you are currently having with someone. What is more important to you right now than restoring *that* relationship?

Sin destroys relationship

All ethical discussions in Christianity must start with the basic problem contained in the story of man's fall into sin.[7] At one point we were without sin, but we became sinners by choosing for ourselves right and wrong, good and evil. Genesis 3 defines sin as man choosing for himself a value system different from God's.

Adam and Eve were placed in the Garden and given only one prohibition. They were told not to eat from the Tree of the Knowledge of Good and Evil. There was nothing magical about the tree or its fruit. The fruit of that particular tree was symbolic of the choice they had to make; a choice that is not unlike the choices we all make. Adam and Eve were given the option of obeying God or disobeying him. They could accept and live with God's value system, or reject it and create their own value systems. Sin is choosing your own value system and rejecting God's. Any value system that acts in a way different from God's value system is sinful.

This was the case with Adam and Eve in the Garden. In order to have the supposed benefits of the fruit,[8] their relationship with God first had to be severed. You do the exact same thing each time you say, "I must follow my wisdom and have the satisfaction of my desires." The value system of God is replaced with a value system that benefits you. The essence of idolatry is pursuing your own desires rather than accepting God's values in your relationships. You turn to idols, along with their value systems and definitions of good, in order to obtain what you want.

The act of eating was not moral, but choosing to eat what God had forbidden was a moral issue. If God had not prohibited *that* tree, they would not have been guilty when they ate from it. But breaking the commandment was not even the real issue. The issue for Adam and

---

7. Genesis 1-3

8. Genesis 3:6 So when the woman saw that the tree was good for food, and that it was a delight to the eyes, and that the tree was to be desired to make one wise, she took of its fruit and ate, and she also gave some to her husband who was with her, and he ate.

Eve was the rejection of the Person behind the commandment. They rejected relationship with God when they chose to live by their own value system. You cannot reject the commandment of God without also rejecting relationship with God; they are inseparable concepts.

Adam and Eve's children continued in sin even though they did not break specific rules and laws given by God, because the nature of sin is not so much a law being broken as a *relationship* with the Lawmaker being broken. Relationship with God is broken when your value system does not match God's, even if you are ignorant of how your values differ from his.

Once Adam and Eve chose to abandon God's value system and replace it with their own, their relationship with one another began to crumble. They exhibited the classic symptoms of relational failure. They immediately began hiding from one another and from God.[9]

When they ceased loving God, they ceased loving one another. When they rejected God's value system, they instantly moved from a value system that served others to a value system that served self. Any act that puts love of self before love of God will affect all other relationships.

Death is relational

The relational consequences of Adam and Eve's sin were immediate. They experienced loss of relationship with God and with each other. Biblically, loss of relationship is described as death. And that day they surely died.[10] Relationships begin to die whenever we consider anything more important than God's value system.

New conflicts were created because Adam and Eve began blaming each other for their problems.[11] They introduced new habits of living for self according to their new value systems. Sinful habits reinforce

---

9. Genesis 3:7-8 Then the eyes of both were opened, and they knew that they were naked. And they sewed fig leaves together and made themselves loincloths. And they heard the sound of the Lord God walking in the garden in the cool of the day, and the man and his wife hid themselves from the presence of the Lord God among the trees of the garden.

10. Genesis 2:16-17 And the Lord God commanded the man, saying, "You may surely eat of every tree of the garden, but of the tree of the knowledge of good and evil you shall not eat, for in the day that you eat of it you shall surely die."

11. Genesis 3:12 The man said, "The woman whom you gave to be with me, she gave me fruit of the tree, and I ate."

other sinful values, hindering a return to God's value system. In fact, apart from God's help, it is not possible to fully return.

Paul, after magnificently declaring that he was not ashamed of the Gospel because of its power to save all people, demonstrated that when people reject God, they reject his value system and replace it with their own.[12] The consequence of that rebellion is a corruption of their desires, ultimately ending in relational failure. They are left hating God and hating one another. The Gospel message is the solution to this disaster people bring on themselves.

Sin is our falling short of God's value system. Sin is relational because practicing ungodly values results in pain and injury to others, which affects relationship. Christ's death on the cross not only removes the offense of our actions before God, it also highlights the great difference between God's value system and our own. God's values always benefit others, while sinful values tend to only benefit self.

Fortunately, God did not abandon Adam and Eve after they sinned. He went looking for them in order to restore relationship with them.[13] He then died on the cross to bring complete restoration.

---

12. Romans 1:18-32

13. Genesis 3:8-9 And they heard the sound of the Lord God walking in the garden in the cool of the day, and the man and his wife hid themselves from the presence of the Lord God among the trees of the garden. But the Lord God called to the man and said to him, "Where are you?"

4 Restoring Relationship

Relationships are so precious to God that he is willing to sacrifice and suffer in order to restore, preserve, and maintain them. Our problem is choosing values different from God's. God's solution to this problem is restoring relationship through the death of Christ.[1] If the nature of sin is rejecting God's value system and replacing it with our own, the crucial element in restoring relationship with God becomes knowing his value system and returning to it. The value system of God is sacrificial love for the benefit of others, and it most looks like Jesus dying on the cross.

Christ's death shows us the extent of his love in removing the consequences of our sin without punishing us for what our own actions deserve. However, Christ's death was not merely to pay the penalty for our sin. It does that, but more importantly, it restores our relationship with God. Since we know that relationship is based on a common value system, we know that *Christ's death was intended to move us from our own value systems to his value system.*

A growing relationship involves two people growing together in value system. A person cannot be said to be growing spiritually if his

---

1. 1 John 2:2 He is the propitiation for our sins, and not for ours only but also for the sins of the whole world.

1 John 4:10 In this is love, not that we have loved God but that he loved us and sent his Son to be the propitiation for our sins.

Propitiate is a relational term. It is about appeasing the offended and restoring relationship.

value system is becoming more selfish, because love for God is measured by how much we adopt his value system. When we reject his value system and reject living by it, we reject him and do not love him. *Spiritual growth and relationship with God can only be measured by how much we share his value system.*

Four steps to relational restoration

Like God, we must deal with sin in relationships. Relationships must be so important to us that we become willing to make sacrifices to uphold, preserve, and increase them.[2] If we want to have quality relationships, we must learn as much as we can about how God acts in relationship.

The method God uses to restore us to himself must become our model for restoring relationship with one another. We must follow a multistep process in order to restore relationship once sin has disrupted it. The first two steps must be done by the offender, and the second two by the one offended. The offender must confess and repent, and after that has happened, the offended can forgive and allow reconciliation. It does not matter if the relationship is between you and God or you and another person: these four steps must be followed for the relationship to be restored.

Step 1: Confession

The first step that the sinner must take is to identify his own selfishness as it relates to his value system. A person cannot be forgiven unless he first agrees he has done something wrong.[3] Confession is an agreement about what the offense is. God requires confession to ensure we understand the difference between our value system and his. We must acknowledge that our actions were unloving, unsacrificial, and selfish.

Our motive in requiring confession from sinners is the same. There can be no restoration of relationship until there is first an agreement on value system, otherwise the conflict will continue. Love desires that the sinner change and knows that it can only happen if the sinner realizes the source of the problem.

2. 1 Peter 4:8 Above all, keep loving one another earnestly, since love covers a multitude of sins.

3. 1 John 1:9 If we confess our sins, he is faithful and just to forgive us our sins and to cleanse us from all unrighteousness.

Step 2: Repentance

Repentance is a change of mind about, and alteration of, our value systems. The essence of repentance is facing a sinful desire and seeing the ugliness of it. But it is more than acknowledging the problem; it is working to fix it. Repentance is rejecting our own value systems and adopting God's value system.

God requires that we repent to enter into his Kingdom because relationship is based on a common value system. Unless we change, we cannot be restored to relationship with him. Rejecting God's value system is rejecting relationship with God. It is two ways of saying the same thing. He requires repentance to ensure we are ready and willing to move from our sinful values to his value system of sacrificial love.

Many people do not like the relational results of their value systems, but they still refuse to change. Repentance sees that the desires and their results are inseparable, and that together they are destructive. A change in value system is the only way to produce a change in desire and bring relational harmony.

Godly relationships are based on sharing God's value system, and sin is an action against those relationships. For the relationship to be restored, repentance must occur because repentance is the change in the sinner toward the value system of the one offended. Without repentance, the sinner does not acknowledge that damage was caused by his value system, and the two parties cannot move closer to each other because they continue to have a difference in value system.

Though God's value system requires that we forgive others, forgiveness is limited only to the repentant. While we may have to wait for someone to repent, we do not wait with anger or bitterness. We wait lovingly, longing for that person to change and be restored. Jesus said, "If your brother sins, rebuke him, and if he repents, forgive him."[4] Note the condition. This is the same requirement God has for forgiving us. We must repent in order to be forgiven.

Why do we only forgive the repentant? The reason is simple. In order for the relationship to be restored through forgiveness, the sinner must first be willing to change his value system. If the sinner will not acknowledge that the problem in the relationship flowed from his value system, the relationship will never proceed past this point of dif-

---

4. Luke 17:3

ference. Relationships are built on common values, and the choice to live by a different value is a choice to limit the relationship.

Step 3: Forgiveness

Once there is agreement on value system, forgiveness removes the guilt of the offense. Forgiveness is not holding the penalty for someone's actions against them. If an action flowing from someone's selfish value system led to insult or injury of another, the injured person will not punish the sinner for those actions. Forgiveness is recognizing the source of the problem—the sinner's value system—and not holding him responsible for the result of it, especially in terms of relationship. When we forgive like God, we choose not to allow a person's *previous* value system to stand in the way of the *current* relationship.

Forgiveness is not optional, it is obligatory. You must forgive others if God has forgiven you[5] because if you are unwilling to forgive the repentant, it proves that you yourself have not adopted God's value system. It means there is something in you (unforgiveness) that you must repent of in order to be restored to relationship with God. It means you have a log in your own eye while grumbling about the speck in someone else's.[6]

God takes forgiveness so seriously that he declared it unforgivable to be unforgiving.[7] Why is God so serious about our forgiving others? Because it is one of the clearest demonstrations that we have adopted his value system and that we are now forgivers as he is.

God will not forgive your sin if you do not forgive others. God values forgiveness so highly that he was willing to die. How can you have fellowship with God unless you value forgiveness as highly as he does? When you are unwilling to forgive, you demonstrate how misaligned your value system is to God's.

Forgiveness is not only a matter of obedience, but also a matter of Christ-likeness. It is not based on emotional feelings; it is an act

5. Colossians 3:13 Bear with each other and forgive whatever grievances you may have against one another. Forgive as the Lord forgave you.

Ephesians 4:32 Be kind and compassionate to one another, forgiving each other, just as in Christ God forgave you.

6. Matthew 7:1-5

7. Matthew 6:14-15 For if you forgive men when they sin against you, your heavenly Father will also forgive you. But if you do not forgive men their sins, your Father will not forgive your sins.

of your will. It is choosing to be like God and living his value system. Forgiveness is not how you feel about what happened; it is how you choose to treat the person you forgive. You must now be the sacrificial lover and become like Christ on the cross, taking the injury of the offense on yourself, and releasing the offender from his debt.

Even as God never forgets what was done when he forgives us, you may not forget what was done to you. But forgiveness is not forgetting; it is choosing not to punish someone for what they have done, in order that relationship might be restored. This is how you can know that you have done your part in forgiving. If you continue to disrupt the relationship after someone has repented, then you have not forgiven and you are not living like Christ.

When you focus on an offense for which repentance has occurred, and use it against someone in a relationally damaging way, you are sinning. You must not take revenge for what was done. You must not replay the history of wrongs done by the other person. You must not gossip to others about the offense in order to hurt the other person. You must not dwell on the offense done to you, but rather dwell on the change in the sinner. This last point is crucial in preventing you from becoming bitter over something done to you.

Relationships are doomed if the participants are unwilling to forgive. Once one or both individuals cease to be forgiving, the relationship begins to deteriorate. Eventually, unforgiveness will become bitterness; and once bitterness overwhelms them, the relationship will come to an end. It does not matter whether the relationship is between husband and wife, parent and child, or a person and God—bitterness, regardless of the source, drives people apart.

Forgiveness is fundamental to Christ-likeness. You cannot have one without the other. The cross is all about forgiveness and relationship. Unless you are forgiving, you are not like Christ.

Step 4: Reconciliation

Once the obstacles (sin, differing value systems, and guilt) are removed, the two people can advance in their relationship. If true repentance and forgiveness have transpired, the relationship will be better than it was before.

When a person repents and changes his value system, it becomes easier to forget the sting of the offense against us. Our emotions more readily respond when we have the joy of seeing a sinner transformed to Christ-likeness. It also becomes less difficult to ask others to forgive us once we admit our fault and desire to change. It is even easier when we are convinced that they will forgive us as God forgives, and seek to love us as much as he does.

Clarifying forgiveness

We are commanded by God to forgive, and forgiving clearly reveals our progress in adopting God's value system. Unfortunately, forgiveness is often misunderstood by those in the Church.

A commonly held view of forgiveness tends to deal with sin in a one-sided manner. For example, a husband does something sinful but his wife "forgives" by putting the matter out of mind and acting as though it never happened. Although we might choose to do this if an issue is insignificant enough to us, it does not express the idea of forgiveness described in the Bible.

To look at this idea from another angle, imagine a child who has disobeyed his parent. His father had given clear instruction and the child willfully disobeyed. Since the father's role is to impress his value system on the child,[8] when the child refuses to adopt his parent's values, it hinders or damages the relationship.

Because the matter of parenting is not insignificant, and since the parent has given instruction that the child has willfully disobeyed, the child must change. If the father simply acts as though the disobedience never occurred, he is raising a child that does not share his value system and is endangering their future relationship.

This brings us back to dealing with sin and forgiveness in the manner described in the Bible. The child must confess his sin, acknowledging the difference between his value system and his father's. The child must also repent; that is, he must change from what he previously valued to what his father values.

At this point, the father can now forgive the child's behavior and the relationship can be restored. No longer will the child's previous value system and resultant actions affect the current relationship. If the child does not confess and repent, it proves that he does not value what his parent values. Attempting to have restored relationship without an agreement on values is a mistake that can weaken relationship

8. Ideally, the father's value system is modeled after God's.

in the long term.

Note that at no point was the father seeking to "get even" with the child, nor was he holding a grudge against him. Even during the child's disobedience, the father sought to change the child and restore him to relationship. Biblical forgiveness is never vindictive, even when it must wait for a sinner to repent. Forgiveness is not an emotion or feeling; it is part of a *process* of relational restoration. Forgiveness is releasing someone from the *relational* consequences of what his actions deserve.[9]

While we wait for someone to confess and repent, we must do no wrong to him. If we do anything that "makes him pay" for what he has done, we will be unable to truly forgive him when he comes asking for forgiveness.[10] "An eye for an eye and a tooth for a tooth" leaves no room for forgiveness. You must keep available the possibility to forgive someone fully by not doing anything relationally damaging to that other person while you wait for his or her heart to change. All that you withhold are the words, "I forgive you." Biblical forgiveness does not allow you to act against the sinner after *or before* he has asked forgiveness. You may never harbor negative feelings nor seek to hurt the other for what he has done.

For example, if you sin against me and I take revenge against you without waiting for you to repent and ask forgiveness, my sinful response precludes me from being able to sincerely and sacrificially forgive you. Once I have "made you pay," whether physically or verbally, I can never forgive you as God has forgiven me. I can never take one hundred percent of the loss upon myself.

A non-biblical idea of forgiveness does not deal with the problem in the relationship. It may not "get even" but neither does it work toward resolving the difference in value system in order to restore and build relationship. Godly forgiveness seeks to fix the problem—not avoid it. Avoiding the problem often results in an explosion once the

9. Sinful actions might result in other consequences beyond the relational element. If a person commits a crime, he may be forgiven by the victim but still must face consequences for his actions. A child may be forgiven for his rebellion, but still may face predetermined consequences for that rebellion. The relationship is restored, but the child knew the consequences and chose those along with his sinful behavior.

10. Parental discipline of a child is not vindictive but instructive. It attempts to impress on the child the seriousness of holding sinful values in the heart. Forgiveness is relational and does not necessarily absolve a child from corrective discipline.

"forgiver" becomes exhausted by the sinner's behavior. Rather than building stronger relationships, a wrong idea of forgiveness allows sin to continue damaging the relationship.

If you compare both ideas of forgiveness, you will see that practically they look the same. The wronged person does no evil to the sinner and harbors no negative attitudes and feelings toward him. However, only biblical forgiveness seeks to restore and improve relationship. God requires that we seek relationship and forgive as he has forgiven us. He requires we follow his model of forgiveness and not the one the world defines.

Relationship between the Father and the Son

In becoming sin, Jesus removed the problem in our relationship with the Father.[11] Think of it like this: he who knew no sin in relationship accepted a break in relationship with his Father so that our relationship with the Father could be restored. Jesus was willing to experience separation from his Father, temporarily breaking their perfect relationship, because of our sin.

Our great need led to his great sacrifice. Sacrifice can always be measured by the level of need: the greater the need, the greater the sacrifice required to help. Indeed, our need was great to require the God who dwells in perfect, eternal relationship to be willing to break it in order to restore relationship with us. We cannot measure the enormity of that sacrifice.

But God the Father could not remain out of relationship with his Son, because at no time did Christ ever have a value system different from his Father's. Even though he willingly endured the punishment for our rebellion, his relationship with the Father could not be permanently severed because their relationship always was, and always will be, based on a perfectly identical value system. Even at the cross they both were expressing sacrificial love.

We can now see that the Gospel is the key to our returning to God's value system and having relationship with him restored. Not only is God's value system revealed most clearly by Christ dying on the cross, but one of the fundamental elements in believing the Gospel is adopting God's value system. The loss of glory at the Fall can only be undone

11. 2 Corinthians 5:18-21 For our sake he made him to be sin who knew no sin, so that in him we might become the righteousness of God.

when we stop living Adam and Eve's choice of rejecting God's value system, and instead begin to mold our lives according to God's value system.[12]

Christ-likeness restores relationship

In human relationships restoration only occurs when an agreement is made over values. A husband and wife cannot resolve their conflicts until they first conclude how they should live and treat one another. Once they agree, they are able to change toward that value system and move relationally toward each other. As long as differences remain over values they can never be fully reconciled.

The same is true between us and God. We cannot be reconciled to God unless our value systems change. He is not going to change his values, or "see our point of view" and adopt our value systems. He paid too high a price to allow us to stay in our sin. Our transformation back into the image of Christ begins by our adopting his value system and relinquishing our own. Common value system is the only basis for relationship with Christ.

We cannot keep living the same old value system if we have been reconciled to God. If we adopt his value system, it will be lived out in our human relationships. When we fail in our human relationships it is because we have first failed to adopt God's value system in that area of failure, and we are still living by our own selfish desires. We must confess we are sinners holding to values that are selfish and not like his. If we confess and repent, we open the door to being transformed through relationship with God.

Your best relationships will revolve around sacrificial love for others. When someone fails to act in love, you have the opportunity to forgive and become a sacrificial lover like God. When you sin, you need to be humble and recognize the source of the problem is your selfish value system, and then seek to change it.

12. 2 Corinthians 3:18 And we all, with unveiled face, beholding the glory of the Lord, are being transformed into the same image from one degree of glory to another. For this comes from the Lord who is the Spirit.

5 Sacrifice Requires Faith

In order to understand the Gospel and God's value system, we must understand faith. A wrong view of faith is detrimental to spiritual life, because one's relationship with God will be hindered by erroneous views. All theology is relational, and relationship with God depends on our ability to trust him. Faith is the trust portion of our relationship with God. Ultimately, *faith is believing the promises of God.*

God values faith in him very highly, and faith is the means by which we honor and please him. Faith is fundamental to Christian living: we cannot receive salvation without it, we cannot have peace with God without it, and we cannot please God without it.[1] However, faith is not only about God being pleased with us. It is the basis for our being pleased with him as well. Without faith it is impossible to have relationship with God.

Throughout the Bible, faith is tied to the story of Abraham. Paul called him the man of faith.[2] Abraham is commended for his faith in Hebrews 11. By studying Abraham, we gain a clear picture of what faith is and how it should operate in our lives. The central element of faith is that it believes the promises of God. Abraham is the man of faith because he believed the promises God made to him.

---

1. Hebrews 11:6 And without faith it is impossible to please him, for whoever would draw near to God must believe that he exists and that he rewards those who seek him.

2. Galatians 3:9

The promises that Abraham believed

Abraham left his home and followed this promise God made to him: "I will make of you a great nation, and I will bless you and make your name great, so that you will be a blessing. I will bless those who bless you, and him who dishonors you I will curse, and in you all the families of the earth shall be blessed."[3] The promise of blessing formed the foundation of Abraham's faith in God.

God then promised Abraham a son through whom he would have descendants as numerous as the stars.[4] Abraham believed the Lord, and God counted it to him as righteousness.[5] This is the first time "believe" is used in the Old Testament, and it is tied to righteousness. For Paul, this became the basis for showing that we are justified before God, not by works of the Law, but by faith in God's promise.[6] Ultimately, we are saved through faith in the salvation promised by Christ, and not by any works that we do.

Later, Abraham was called to practice the covenant of circumcision in faith.[7] When he circumcised his sons it was a sign of his faith. Circumcision demonstrated the parent's faith, not the faith of the child. When Abraham participated in circumcision it was an active demonstration of his belief that God would fulfill his promises to him.

Faith is joy in the promise

Abraham's wife, Sarah, had endured many disappointments in her life. She was not able to bear the children she desired. Besides that, Sarah had to move away from her home and family, travelling with her husband to a distant land. She also had a husband who put himself before her in several circumstances. Finally, she resolved that she would have to share her husband with her servant, Hagar, so that Abraham might have an heir. After this, Hagar's son, Ishmael, brought even more conflict into her home and life.

Sarah did not get her desires according to her own timetable. She finally did get a son, but when she heard the promise that he was com-

---

3. Genesis 12:2-3
4. Genesis 15
5. Genesis 15:6
6. Romans 4
7. Genesis 17

ing, she laughed and was rebuked for it.[8] Her laugh was an act of unbelief, possibly as a response to all her years of disappointment. When we experience disappointment and do not respond to it with faith, we will experience even more disappointment. Disappointment without faith leads to discouragement and depression.

When Abraham heard the promise that he would have a son through Sarah, he also laughed.[9] We know that Abraham's laugh was not a laugh of unbelief because God did not rebuke Abraham as he had Sarah. Abraham's laughter was one of joy;[10] it was a laugh of faith. You either laugh in faith or in unbelief. Those who laugh in faith receive God's promises and blessing. Those who laugh in unbelief receive rebuke.

Abraham was glad and laughed. He believed this was the coming fulfillment of the first promise God had made to him: that he would become a great nation and all the families of the earth would be blessed through him. Although Abraham's faith was evident before Isaac was born, the most significant example of it came after Isaac's birth.

The action that proved Abraham believed

Abraham's faith had yet to be fully tested. After telling Abraham that Isaac was the one through whom God's promises would be fulfilled,[11] God asked Abraham to sacrifice this same son.[12]

> *Was not our ancestor Abraham considered righteous for what he did when he offered his son Isaac on the altar? You see that his faith and his actions were working together, and his faith was made complete by what he did. And the scripture was fulfilled*

---

8. Genesis 18:10-15

9. Genesis 17:15-17 God also said to Abraham, "As for Sarai your wife, you are no longer to call her Sarai; her name will be Sarah. I will bless her and will surely give you a son by her. I will bless her so that she will be the mother of nations; kings of peoples will come from her." Abraham fell facedown; he laughed and said to himself, "Will a son be born to a man a hundred years old? Will Sarah bear a child at the age of ninety?"

10. John 8:56 Your father Abraham rejoiced at the thought of seeing my day; he saw it and was glad.

11. Genesis 21:12

12. Genesis 22:1-2 After these things God tested Abraham and said to him, "Abraham!" And he said, "Here am I." He said, "Take your son, your only son Isaac, whom you love, and go to the land of Moriah, and offer him there as a burnt offering on one of the mountains of which I shall tell you."

that says, "Abraham believed God, and it was credited to him as righteousness," and he was called God's friend. You see that a person is justified by what he does and not by faith alone.[13]

God tested[14] Abraham by giving him two different revelations that appeared to conflict. First, he received a child who was born to be the means of fulfilling God's promises to him. Second, he was ordered to sacrifice that child before the promise was fulfilled. In spite of the conflict, Abraham chose to obey and not turn away from God's voice commanding him.

How could God fulfill his promise if Isaac were dead? Yet God said to kill him. Abraham chose to let God sort out the discrepancy. The offering of his son proved the greatness of his faith in God's promise, "through Isaac shall your offspring be named,"[15] the very promise tied to his justification.[16] Even though God made a promise to Abraham and followed it up with a command that seemed to destroy the promise, Abraham was nevertheless confident that God would keep his promises.

Abraham obeyed God because he believed that God could raise the dead.[17] We know this because he was willing to sacrifice his son, yet believed he would return with his son.[18] Abraham's faith in God's promise was so strong that he believed even death could not hinder God from keeping it. Abraham believed in a God who could and would raise the dead in order to keep his promise.

Genuine faith *acts* on the promises of God. Faith is believing something so deeply that it changes the course of your life. Abraham

---

13. James 2:21-24

14. Genesis 22:1

15. Genesis 21:12

16. Genesis 15:4-6 And behold, the word of the Lord came to him: "This man shall not be your heir; your very own son shall be your heir." And he brought him outside and said, "Look toward heaven, and number the stars, if you are able to number them." Then he said to him, "So shall your offspring be." And he believed the Lord, and he counted it to him as righteousness.

17. Hebrews 11:17-19 By faith Abraham, when he was tested, offered up Isaac, and he who had received the promises was in the act of offering up his only son, of whom it was said, "Through Isaac shall your offspring be named." He considered that God was able even to raise him from the dead, from which, figuratively speaking, he did receive him back.

18. Genesis 22:5 Then Abraham said to his young men, "Stay here with the donkey; I and the boy will go over there and worship and come again to you."

had previously left his old life behind, but now he was willing to give up everything, as exemplified through sacrificing his son. Because of God's command, Abraham's faith could only be proved through action. He was clearly ready to go through with the sacrifice, but God intervened at the last moment and stopped him.[19]

Abraham believed the promises of God so deeply that he would give his life for them. Having faith like Abraham's requires that you live in a way that demonstrates you really believe the promise. Saying you believe is not the same as having conduct that demonstrates you believe. You cannot claim to believe God unless your actions prove that you will live and die according to his promises. If you do not rely on a promise, it proves you do not believe it.

Faith believes in resurrection

How do we demonstrate faith in God's promises? If we believe God provides a resurrection for us, and that he is a God who raises the dead, then we will not be afraid to give this life up for others. But if we selfishly cling to this life and that which benefits us without living and giving sacrificially for others, we demonstrate we are not quite sure of resurrection. We hope it will happen and we hope that there is a heaven, but we are not willing to take the risks that faith requires. Faith is willing to sacrifice only when it is confident that God has promised something.

God measures our faith by what we will not withhold from him. When Abraham was willing to offer his precious son, it demonstrated he loved God more than himself. More significantly, Abraham could see his own faith confirmed in what he was willing to do. Abraham revealed faith in the promise of a God who resurrects. Until you face that which you refuse to give God, you cannot enter into his full peace and blessing. Do you love God enough to sacrifice for him? Do you believe his promises enough to offer all that is precious to you for his Kingdom?

Our faith in God's promises is only evident when we live in a way that demonstrates our deep reliance on them. If we really believe that God raises the dead, we will be willing to live our lives in sacrifice for

---

19. Genesis 22:11-12 But the angel of the Lord called to him from heaven and said, "Abraham, Abraham!" And he said, "Here am I." He said, "Do not lay your hand on the boy or do anything to him, for now I know that you fear God, seeing you have not withheld your son, your only son, from me."

others because we know that this life is not the end of our existence. If we live selfish lives, it proves we do not believe God's promises to us. Without actions confirming faith, there is no faith.

We can place our trust in God's promises because he swears by himself to fulfill them.[20] When God makes a promise his entire justice hangs on him keeping his word. If he breaks a promise, then he is a liar and a sinner, and is no better than any of us. All his glory would be swept away if he broke his word *even one time.* One thing you can fully trust that can never be shaken is that God will keep his promises.

What are the promises of God?

God will never break any of his promises, so we can place our confidence in them. Since our whole faith rests on the bedrock of God keeping his word, we must be very sure of what his promises are and are not. Any time we read something in the Bible that seems like an unfulfilled promise, we must consider a few possible explanations:

- The promise was not for me, but for someone else.
- The promise is not for now, but for some other time.
- The promise is not to be taken literally.
- The promise has been taken out of context.
- The text is misunderstood and is not a promise at all.
- The text is misinterpreted and is a promise about something else.
- The promise was not from God, and the text is corrupt or not true.
- God does not keep his promises.

Since these are the possibilities, we must be very sure we have an accurate understanding of who God is and what he has really promised. It would be foolish to rely on a promise you believe is from God when it actually is not. Besides being dangerous, it also gives God a bad name if we claim he promised something when he did no such thing. It also causes people to hate God or blame him when they think he has been unfaithful.

---

20. Genesis 22:15-18 And the angel of the Lord called to Abraham a second time from heaven and said, "By myself I have sworn, declares the Lord, because you have done this and have not withheld your son, your only son, I will surely bless you, and I will surely multiply your offspring as the stars of heaven and as the sand that is on the seashore. And your offspring shall possess the gate of his enemies, and in your offspring shall all the nations of the earth be blessed, because you have obeyed my voice."

This is why we must later examine some "promises" of God that are, in fact, misinterpretations of the biblical text.[21] These misinterpretations are detrimental to faith because people conclude that God does not keep his word and he breaks his promises. In order to trust God enough to live sacrificially for others, we must be able to trust his word and his promises completely. We must believe he has forgiven our sins and restored us to relationship with himself. We must be able to rely on a God who raises the dead, confident that this world is not the end. And we must believe that we will be rewarded not only in this life, but also in the next, for what we do now.

Demonstrating faith within the Kingdom

Faith is a demonstration of trust in God's promises. Unless you believe the promises of God regarding salvation and resurrection, it will be very difficult for you to practice sacrificial love for others. If God does not resurrect you when you lay down your life for another, then you lose everything when you sacrifice. This is precisely why sacrificial love is so difficult for Christians. We have little faith that God rewards and resurrects those who give their lives away for others. We ultimately have little faith in Christ's resurrection and are unsure that he truly is the firstfruits[22] of those raised from the dead.

Faith in God's promises is demonstrated through obedience to Christ's call to be like him: "If anyone would come after me, let him deny himself and take up his cross and follow me."[23] Note that Christ does not ask us to do anything that he himself is not willing to do. He does not call us to sacrifice while avoiding it himself. God's love is most demonstrated by Christ's death on the cross. Our love for God is most demonstrated by our sacrificial love for others. Our faith in eternal life and the blessings of the Kingdom can only be revealed to ourselves, to God, and to others by living a life that looks like Jesus dying on the cross.

> *Whoever loves father or mother more than me is not worthy of me, and whoever loves son or daughter more than me is not worthy of me. And whoever does not take his cross and follow me is not worthy of me. Whoever finds his life will lose it, and*

---

21. See Chapter 29: Prayer and Sacrificial Love

22. 1 Corinthians 15:20 But in fact Christ has been raised from the dead, the firstfruits of those who have fallen asleep.

23. Matthew 16:24

whoever loses his life for my sake will find it.[24]

Faith is your trust that God will do what he says. Faith is your trust that God has raised Christ from the dead and will also raise you. Unwillingness to be sacrificial demonstrates a lack of trust in God, and it reveals how limited your relationship with God truly is.

Faith is believing what God says about your sin—that you are cut off from relationship with him. Faith is believing what he says about judgment—that you are condemned and in need of help. Faith is believing what he says about transformation—that he can save you from yourself. But faith is also the only way to enter the place of transformation. By faith we acknowledge our sin and rejection of God's value system. By faith we recognize God acted to restore us to himself. And by faith we seek to adopt his value system and abandon our own.

This explains why faith is required for salvation. You must believe what God says about you and sin and value systems. Until you desire to be transformed, until you desire to have your value system changed, you cannot enter into relationship with him. Salvation is about value systems. Relationship with God (salvation) is dependent on your desire to change your value system. Believing is not believing *that* he died, but believing *all* he said about his death.

Salvation requires belief that God created you for relationship with him. It requires belief that your relationship with him is dead because you chose a different value system. And it requires belief that relationship with him can be restored only through adopting his value system.

Faith in Christ's death is your belief that it is God's value system you see at the cross. Faith in Christ's death is your belief that your sinful deeds (actions committed according to your rebellious value system) require punishment and rejection. Faith in Christ's death is acknowledging that God rejected his Son so that he might not have to reject you.

It takes great faith for us to give our lives away in sacrificial love for others. It requires that we believe God keeps his promises and that he raises the dead. Until we believe this deeply, we will struggle with sacrificial love for the benefit of others. You must understand this point clearly. The magnitude of it will become clear later when we examine some of Jesus' promises. Your ability to fearlessly follow Christ is directly related to your faith in his authority.

24. Matthew 10:37-39

6 The Law Cannot Transform

Many Christians can easily identify Paul's argument concerning the Law's inability to bring salvation to men because of sin, but he revealed another aspect of the Law's failure in 2 Corinthians 3:7-4:6. In this beautiful passage, Paul discussed the Law's inability to bring transformation to Christ-likeness. Not only does the Law only partially reveal God's value system, it is insufficient to change a person's value system to God's.

A greater glory with Christ

When God made the Old Covenant with the people of Israel, it came with glory since Moses received the Law from God.[1] After speaking with God on Mount Sinai, Moses returned to the people and delivered God's requirements for them. The Israelites saw Moses' face shining, for he had been in the presence of God. Since the Israelites were afraid to look at his face, Moses wore a veil to hide it until the glory faded. This illustrates the whole experience with the Law. Although it came with glory, it came with a fading glory. It came carved

1. 2 Corinthians 3:7-11 Now if the ministry of death, carved in letters on stone, came with such glory that the Israelites could not gaze at Moses' face because of its glory, which was being brought to an end, will not the ministry of the Spirit have even more glory? For if there was glory in the ministry of condemnation, the ministry of righteousness must far exceed it in glory. Indeed, in this case, what once had glory has come to have no glory at all, because of the glory that surpasses it. For if what was being brought to an end came with glory, much more will what is permanent have glory.

on stone and brought condemnation and death to men.

But the New Covenant in the blood of Christ has a greater glory. Its glory does not fade away; it persists. It comes as a ministry of the Spirit and brings righteousness and life. The New Covenant is so glorious that it makes the Old seem dull. Amazingly, some act as if they have a choice in which Covenant they will live under. Although no one now has the option to live under the Old Covenant, people still choose to live by the Old Covenant Law instead of the Covenant that frees us to live by Christ's command to love.

For many, it seems easier to live by the Law. They feel confident that they know all the rules and can immediately scratch from the list anything that does not apply to them. But one day they will find that they did not achieve life by the Law. Although they may have not murdered their neighbor, neither did they really love him. The world is not necessarily a better place because of their existence.

The New Covenant has more glory than the Old because it looks more like God. *The more something looks like the God of glory, the more glorious it is.* The Law had glory because it began to reveal God's glory—his value system—to men. But compared to Christ and all he gives in the Gospel, the Law is dull. The value system of the Kingdom far outshines the value system of the Old Testament Law because by it we know God's sacrificial love for us that allows us to become sacrificial lovers.

The problem with the Law is that it can never make you Christlike. Any benefits gained from it are passing, temporary, and fading. There is no permanent transformation into the glorious likeness of God through it. There is only a reflecting of God's glory.

An unveiling with Christ

Moses veiled his face after delivering God's word to the people so that they would not look at the glory.[2] Although the Old Testament does not explicitly say the shining faded, Paul inferred it. Thus, we

---

2. 2 Corinthians 3:12-17 Since we have such a hope, we are very bold, not like Moses, who would put a veil over his face so that the Israelites might not gaze at the outcome of what was being brought to an end. But their minds were hardened. For to this day, when they read the old covenant, that same veil remains unlifted, because only through Christ is it taken away. Yes, to this day whenever Moses is read a veil lies over their hearts. But when one turns to the Lord, the veil is removed. Now the Lord is the Spirit, and where the Spirit of the Lord is, there is freedom.

have the picture of Moses wearing no veil when he spoke to God, and no veil when he spoke from God to the people. However, he did wear a veil when his face shone and he was *not* delivering God's word.

Every time Moses entered the presence of God, the reflected glory was renewed. When Moses spoke from God, it was right for the Israelites to see the glory because the words he spoke were not his own words. The glory and the words were both God's. When Moses spoke the words of God, he had no need to cover his face. It was only *after* delivering God's message to the people that he covered his face.[3] He did this because the glory was not his own.

The veil's purpose was to *hide* God's glory. A veil remains over the heart of anyone seeking God through the Old Covenant. That veil prevents the glory of Christ in the New Covenant from shining on the heart. The glory of Christ is unable to transform anyone still relying on the Law, and anyone who relies on the Law for transformation will not be changed.

With the Law there is a concealment of the heart that prevents transformation. A man can keep the Law even while harboring evil desires in his heart. But attempting to hide sin under the Law never leads to glory any more than hiding sin by any other means leads to glory. However, one can hide behind the Law, having an appearance of righteousness while remaining untransformed and unglorified.

The Law does not transform people. At best, they become *reflectors* of God's glory, but never *bearers* of his glory. When a person practices the Law, he exhibits qualities of God to the degree he keeps the Law. But those characteristics can be merely external, requiring no internal change. The Law does not change people; obedience to it is merely a reflection of Someone else's glory.

But Christ removes the veil. In fact, only in Christ is it taken away. There is no other means for its removal; one must turn to Christ. Christ *restores* the glory lost at the Fall. The veil that blocked the reflected glory of God on Moses' face still separates Israel from the full glory of God in Christ. When a person remains under Law, the veil that blocks the glory of God prevents him from responding to Christ's glory.

---

3. Exodus 34:34-35 Whenever Moses went in before the Lord to speak with him, he would remove the veil, until he came out. And when he came out and told the people of Israel what he was commanded, the people of Israel would see the face of Moses, that the skin of Moses' face was shining. And Moses would put the veil over his face again, until he went in to speak with him.

Part of the freedom we have is a freedom to approach God. Unlike Moses, who was the only one permitted to approach God, all in Christ can see God and reflect his glory. In the Old Covenant, only one person beheld the glory of God with an unveiled face. In the New Covenant, all participants behold the glory of God.

A transformation with Christ

Christians are not glorified because they are better reflectors of glory. Christians are not even glorified by their possession of a value system that is far superior to the Law. They are glorified because they are not merely *reflecting* God's glory, but are *transformed* to the same glory God possesses. We not only reflect glory, but shine it ourselves.[4]

This is why we need not cover our faces. Moses covered his face because the glory he reflected was not his own. We need not cover our faces because the glory we have and shine *is our own.* It is our transformation into the likeness of Christ, having adopted his value system in our hearts. This is why Paul said that he does not need to hide anything, as with a veil. When a person is transformed to God's value system there is nothing to hide.

Furthermore, it is our hearts that reflect Christ, not our faces. In other words, the glory is not something external to us. The inner person, with its character and values, changes. This is a significant difference from only having a glowing countenance.

The Lord is the Spirit who gives us freedom from our bondage to the Law. With it he gives us boldness because we have a hope in the New Covenant of something that endures. A replacement for the Gospel will never come, because there is no greater value system than what

---

4. 2 Corinthians 3:18-4:6 And we all, with unveiled face, beholding the glory of the Lord, are being transformed into the same image from one degree of glory to another. For this comes from the Lord who is the Spirit. Therefore, having this ministry by the mercy of God, we do not lose heart. But we have renounced disgraceful, underhanded ways. We refuse to practice cunning or to tamper with God's word, but by the open statement of the truth we would commend ourselves to everyone's conscience in the sight of God. And even if our gospel is veiled, it is veiled only to those who are perishing. In their case the god of this world has blinded the minds of the unbelievers, to keep them from seeing the light of the gospel of the glory of Christ, who is the image of God. For what we proclaim is not ourselves, but Jesus Christ as Lord, with ourselves as your servants for Jesus' sake. For God, who said, "Let light shine out of darkness," has shone in our hearts to give the light of the knowledge of the glory of God in the face of Jesus Christ.

God exhibited on the cross. God will never supersede it with something else. He allows us and wants us to reflect his glory, but it is also our own glory as our hearts are transformed into his likeness through his value system, and not through the external Law.

No need for the Law

Paul taught that attempting to make Christians follow the Law is a great deceit.[5] He said this because he had a better ministry and a greater privilege than Moses. He also had a better message than Moses—grace rather than Law. Anyone who promotes living by the Law is more interested in proclaiming self rather than Christ.

Paul never made the Gentile Christians obey the Law of Moses. If he had, he would have been leaving people with the veil. He did not want to make Gentiles follow the Law because he knew it did not have the power to help people overcome sin. He had experienced firsthand its failure to transform. He knew that when he lived under the Law—fulfilling it as well as any other—he still harbored murder in his heart. He was deceived—cut off from God while thinking he knew him.

When a person is unwilling to accept the Gospel, it is because unbelief continues to veil it. Those who cannot see the glory of Christ in those who have been transformed by the Gospel reveal that they have been blinded. Paul's experience was dramatically illustrated in his Damascus road experience.[6] There he literally saw the glory of Christ. The light of Christ shone in his heart and, as Paul believed, the veil was removed and his blindness receded. He moved from darkness to light by the knowledge of Christ.

Paul desired to help others find the truth of Christ, the glory of Christ, and the light of Christ. He would never lead a person to the Law because the Law offered nothing compared to what Christ gave freely: the power of life, freedom, and love.

The reason the cross of Christ will never be superseded is because it is the fullest expression of God's value system. Throughout time, and as recorded in the Bible, God progressively revealed his value system; and along with it, more and more of his identity. But at the cross, the full glory of who God is was made manifest. We need not emulate the partial revelation of God found in the Law since we can be trans-

---

5. 2 Corinthians 4:1-6
6. Acts 9

formed by the Spirit into the full revelation found in Christ's love.

The glory we receive from Christ, his likeness, is an unfading and enduring glory. It does not come through the Law, but through the Spirit as we adopt Christ's value system. The Law can only reflect God's glory as we do it. It looks like God's glory, but it is only a reflected glory. When our hearts are transformed into the likeness of Christ, as our hearts become filled with sacrificial love for others, we become glorious in and of ourselves. We are glorified and transformed into the likeness of God in a way that no laws or rules can ever achieve.

Only a change of value system in the heart can bring to an individual a glory that is the likeness of God. External rules can at best make us *look* like God, but they can never truly change us to *be* like God. We can appear to have God's values by practicing the Law, but we only truly have God's values when our hearts are transformed into Christ-likeness by adopting his value system of sacrificial love for others.

This ultimately is the failure of Law and works. They can never make us be who we are intended to be. They can make us look good on the outside, but they cannot make us good on the inside. They can only partially reveal God's glory to us, and they can never transform us into that glory. Only the Spirit does that as we adopt God's value system. Only then are we truly like him and shine a glory of our own. Without internal goodness, we can never have relationship with God.

God's value system becomes the fount for all our living and loving. We no longer rely on the Law and rules for determining what is goodness and holiness. Goodness and holiness flow from our being like God in our hearts. There is nothing we will do opposed to God if we are practicing his value system of sacrificial love.

Part 2: The Message of the King

7 The King and His Covenant

In realizing that the main focus of Jesus' teaching was his Kingdom, we can gain correct insight into all he said and did. That which appears mysterious or seems difficult to understand becomes clear once we regard it as instruction about the nature of the Kingdom. Approaching the book of Matthew with this in mind sheds new light on each passage.[1] While studying each section and teaching, we must consider how it relates to the King and his Kingdom.

Matthew is the first book in what we call the New Testament in our Bibles. We need to be clear on the meaning of the two parts of our Bibles called the Old and New Testaments. A different translation of the word "testament" is "covenant." The Old Covenant and the New Covenant would be the different ways of describing the two parts of the Bible. Everyone familiar with the Last Supper should know that there is a New Covenant.[2]

So what is a covenant? A covenant is a promise made between two people (or groups) to fulfill the obligations specified in the covenant.

1. Each Gospel account in the New Testament has its own theme. Each theme guided the author to include or omit material from the life of Christ. It also guided the order and presentation of his material. What sets the Gospel of Matthew apart is the theme of Christ as King of the Kingdom of God. Everything in the book of Matthew follows this one theme from the beginning to the end of Jesus' earthly ministry. Every recorded teaching and action is about the King and his Kingdom.

2. 1 Corinthians 11:25 In the same way also he took the cup, after supper, saying, "This cup is the new covenant in my blood. Do this, as often as you drink it, in remembrance of me."

Along with the positive benefits of the promise, certain penalties might be listed in the covenant for those who violate it. It is like a legal contract with penalties for breaking it.

When God makes a covenant with us, he requires that we have faith that he will keep his part of it. We can never enter into a covenant with God without believing the promises that accompany the covenant. Since covenants revolve around promises, one could almost describe the Bible as having the two parts named the Old Promise and the New Promise.

God's covenants often have two parts to them: an unconditional part that God will do, and a conditional part that the people in the covenant must do. We can be sure that God will keep his part, for if God should break a promise, then everything we believe about God is suspect. Our whole view of God in Christianity rests on the fact that God is honest and keeps his word.

Our part of the covenant can only be done through faith. Faith believes and enters into the covenant with God. Faith is also necessary for us to continue in the covenant because we must keep the conditions of the covenant.

Two of the most significant biblical covenants God made were with Abraham and David. Both men lived long before Christ, but the promises God made to them anticipated the New Covenant that Christ instituted.

The Abrahamic Covenant

When God called Abraham to leave his land and follow him, he promised that he would bless all nations through Abraham.[3] He also promised to give Abraham descendants as numerous as the stars.[4] It was at this point that Abraham believed God, and it was reckoned to him as righteousness.[5] God then made a covenant with Abraham in

---

3. Genesis 12:2-3 And I will make of you a great nation, and I will bless you and make your name great, so that you will be a blessing. I will bless those who bless you, and him who dishonors you I will curse, and in you all the families of the earth shall be blessed.

4. Genesis 15:5 And he brought him outside and said, "Look toward heaven, and number the stars, if you are able to number them." Then he said to him, "So shall your offspring be."

5. Genesis 15:6 And he believed the Lord, and he counted it to him as righteousness.

which he promised to care for his descendants and give them the land of Canaan.

The final aspect of the covenant was something that Abraham and his progeny were required to do, and it was instituted when God promised to give Abraham a son through Sarah. God gave Abraham the sign of circumcision for the covenant[6] and told him that the covenant would be fulfilled through Isaac.[7] The covenant had the unconditional part of God's blessing, but also a conditional part in which the people exercised faith by using the sign of circumcision to confirm their participation in the covenant.

The Davidic Covenant

The story of the Davidic Covenant began with David's desire to build a house, or temple, for God.[8] God responded to David's desire by telling him that David would not build a house for God, but that God would build a house for David. That is, God would give David an everlasting kingdom with a son always on the throne.

This covenant had an unconditional part in which God promised David an enduring kingdom, but it also had a conditional part for David's royal line.[9] Each son had to adhere to the value system of David;[10] each one had to be a man who pursued God as David did.[11] The king must be good, as David his father was; and if he were not, God could remove him for doing evil.

---

6. Genesis 17:10 This is my covenant, which you shall keep, between me and you and your offspring after you: Every male among you shall be circumcised.

7. Genesis 15:4; 17:16; 21:12

8. 2 Samuel 7

9. When kings were anointed at the temple by the priests, they stood before two bronze pillars. Solomon named the pillars Jachin ("he established") and Boaz ("by him he is mighty"), which may have signified God's establishment of the Davidic dynasty and the new king's need for reliance on God.

10. 2 Samuel 7:14 I will be to him a father, and he shall be to me a son. When he commits iniquity, I will discipline him with the rod of men, with the stripes of the sons of men…

11. David became the standard by which all other Judaic kings were measured.

1 Kings 11:4 For when Solomon was old his wives turned away his heart after other gods, and his heart was not wholly true to the Lord his God, as was the heart of David his father.

1 Kings 15:3 And he walked in all the sins that his father did before him, and his heart was not wholly true to the Lord his God, as the heart of David his father.

There was another very significant change in Israel with the coming of the Davidic Covenant: the king became the representative of the people before God. If the king did what was right, God blessed the nation. If the king did what was wrong, God punished the nation.[12] Eventually, the last king of Judah was removed because of rebellion, and the kingdom was destroyed by the Babylonians.[13]

In these two covenants, God made promises to Abraham and to David because of who those two men were: those promises were unconditional. But the descendants of Abraham and David could only inherit the blessings of each covenant if they did something that demonstrated their own faith in the covenant. Abraham's descendents needed to practice circumcision, whereas David's sons needed to recognize that God was their Father and adopt his value system.[14]

The New Covenant, the New Promise

When Jesus Christ arrived, he came as the fulfillment of both the promise made to Abraham and the promise made to David. He came as the blessing for all nations, and he also came as the new King. As King, he stands before God representing all of the people in his Kingdom. Since the actions of the King affect only those in his Kingdom, we must be part of Christ's Kingdom if he is to represent us before God. And, like the sons of David, we also must adopt the value system of the King in whose covenant we have entered.

The descendants of Abraham and David could only receive the blessings of God's promise by faithfully keeping the covenant. In the first, it was faith expressed through circumcision. In the second, it was faith expressed through adopting the value system of David.

The New Covenant is a new promise made between God the Father and God the Son. Everyone who desires to enter into the blessings of the New Covenant must first believe in the promise made by

---

12. Prior to this, the people were dealt with collectively under the Mosaic Covenant. This is explained more fully in the Appendix: Justification, Sanctification, and Glorification.

13. 2 Kings 25

14. This is initially shown in Solomon's prayer and God's response (1 Kings 3) along with statements commending or condemning kings (e.g. 1 Kings 6:12 Concerning this house that you are building, if you will walk in my statutes and obey my rules and keep all my commandments and walk in them, then I will establish my word with you, which I spoke to David your father.).

the Father to the Son. Faith results in righteousness (as in the case of Abraham) and reception of the benefits of the righteous King (as in the case of David representing the people). God does not treat us according to what our own actions deserve, but by the actions of our King, the One who sits on David's throne.

Jesus came to institute the New Covenant, as well as to fulfill the covenants made with Abraham and David. This should not surprise us since Matthew intended we understand this from the start. He began his book by deliberately connecting Jesus Christ with these two previous covenants.

> *The book of the genealogy of Jesus Christ, the son of David, the son of Abraham.*[15]

Son of God and son of David

Everything in the Book of Matthew is about Jesus being the King of God's Kingdom. For us to properly understand any part of the book, we must be careful to examine it with that particular focus. It is impossible to miss that Jesus is first of all King by birth, noticeably born in Bethlehem, the ancestral town of David.

The identity of Jesus is vital to whether or not he has a right to become King. Jesus is the son of Mary by physical birth, but also the son of Joseph by legal descent, and thus heir to the throne of David.[16] But the most crucial element is that he is also the Son of God by preexistence. Jesus comes as the King of the Kingdom of God.

Even the name of the King is significant. "Jesus" is the Greek form of the Hebrew name "Joshua" which means "YHWH[17] is salvation" or "YHWH saves." Jesus[18] is the one who would bring the salvation

---

15. Matthew 1:1

16. Matthew 1:18-20 Now the birth of Jesus Christ took place in this way. When his mother Mary had been betrothed to Joseph, before they came together she was found to be with child from the Holy Spirit. And her husband Joseph, being a just man and unwilling to put her to shame, resolved to divorce her quietly. But as he considered these things, behold, an angel of the Lord appeared to him in a dream, saying, "Joseph, son of David, do not fear to take Mary as your wife, for that which is conceived in her is from the Holy Spirit."

17. YHWH is the Name of God as revealed in the Old Testament, often translated LORD.

18. Matthew 1:21 She will bear a son, and you shall call his name Jesus, for he will save his people from their sins.

promised by YHWH in the Old Testament.[19]

Immanuel

Jesus was also to be known by the name Immanuel.[20] The name Immanuel is tied to the Davidic Covenant and comes from a prophecy in Isaiah 6-12 where we read about a trying time in the history of Judah. God had pronounced a judgment against the land because of sin.[21] The people were to be sent into exile, but a portion of them, a remnant like a stump from a cut down tree, would remain.[22]

The prophecy outlined the following events: Although the kingdoms of Syria and Israel were threatening Judah, Judah was not to be afraid.[23] Rather, Judah was being given a chance to learn and to choose good while rejecting evil. By the time Isaiah's son Immanuel reached the age given in the prophecy, Assyria would sweep through the land.[24]

Finally, the prophecy declared that one day a child would be born as the Davidic heir,[25] the Messiah, and the righteous Branch out of the stump who would restore Israel.[26] All would rejoice in God the Savior in that day.[27] The prophecy of Immanuel was about a new King in Judah who would bring God's salvation. He would not be like the ungodly kings that precipitated the Babylonian captivity.

> *For to us a child is born, to us a son is given; and the government shall be upon his shoulder, and his name shall be called Wonderful Counselor, Mighty God, Everlasting Father, Prince of Peace. Of the increase of his government and of peace there will be no end, on the throne of David and over his kingdom, to establish*

19. Psalm 130:8 And he [YHWH] will redeem Israel from all his iniquities.

20. Matthew 1:23 "Behold, the virgin shall conceive and bear a son, and they shall call his name Immanuel" (which means, God with us).

21. Isaiah 6

22. Jesus specifically referred to this judgment with regard to his speaking in parables to the people (Matthew 13:14). He spoke to the people in parables so they would not understand his teaching unless they came to him for greater clarification. Those who truly sought him would gain spiritual understanding, while those interested only in food or miracles would hear but not understand.

23. Isaiah 7

24. Isaiah 8

25. Isaiah 9

26. Isaiah 11

27. Isaiah 12

> *it and to uphold it with justice and with righteousness from this time forth and forevermore. The zeal of the Lord of hosts will do this.*[28]

It is very important for us to notice who accepted Jesus as King while he was still an infant. The Gentile Magi came and accepted Christ as the new King, whereas the Jewish leaders rejected him.[29] This foreshadowed what would happen throughout the book of Matthew and on into the book of Acts.

The story of Jesus' birth continues with a comparison between him, the rightful King, and Herod, king of the Jews, who was not even a Jew himself. Herod received his position from the Romans, but Jesus received his from God. Jesus would be revealed as a loving sacrificer, whereas Herod was an evil murderer.[30] We are to be very aware of the difference in these two kings and their value systems.

The end of bondage

Matthew continues with two stunning quotations from the Old Testament and applies them to the birth of Christ. These texts take on new significance once applied to the birth of Christ, and they reveal the depth of Matthew's understanding of the Old Testament.

The tears of Rachel[31] are significant because they marked the beginning of the Jewish exile to Babylon, which, incidentally, was also the end of the Davidic kingdom. The tears are mentioned here in the New Testament because they marked the *ending* of the exile now that the new King had come. The restoration of the Davidic throne was in progress. The tears of Rachel were in the writings of the prophet Jeremiah who said that after the tears, God would institute the New Covenant.[32] Thus, the weeping could now stop because the Son of David had come, and with him, the New Covenant.

"Out of Egypt I called my son"[33] is also a very interesting prophecy applied to Jesus. Matthew's point is that Jesus is the true Israel; he is

---

28. Isaiah 9:6-7

29. Matthew 2:1-12

30. Matthew 2:16

31. Matthew 2:18 "A voice was heard in Ramah, weeping and loud lamentation, Rachel weeping for her children; she refused to be comforted, because they are no more."

32. Jeremiah 31

33. Matthew 2:15

the true Son of God. Jesus is not like the rebellious Israel in the Old Testament who came under judgment for sin. By the time of Christ, Israel was no longer an independent nation. Israel was still being ruled by foreigners because of rebellion, still in a form of Egyptian bondage, and still in a form of exile even in her homeland. The people needed to repent and obey God as their King.

Jesus came to free his people from the source of their bondage. Israel was still in bondage because of her sin and rebellion against God's value system. Jesus came to deal a final blow to the source of that rebellion.

The Nazarene

Finally, Jesus would be called a Nazarene:

> *And he went and lived in a city called Nazareth, that what was spoken by the prophets might be fulfilled: "He shall be called a Nazarene."*[34]

Since there is no specific Old Testament text that can be identified in this quote, Matthew is very careful to write "prophets" instead of naming a specific prophet. He intended to express a general idea conveyed by many different prophets.

Being called a Nazarene foretold the rejection of Jesus as King. He was not raised affiliated with David, but with antagonism because of his home of Nazareth. He was an outcast, rejected, and was not recognized for who he truly was. We see this in the words of Nathaniel when he asked, "Can anything good come out of Nazareth?"[35] We also see it when the Jews spoke derisively of the followers of Christ by calling them the sect of the Nazarenes.[36] This is in line with what the prophet Isaiah wrote:

> *For he grew up before him like a young plant, and like a root out of dry ground; he had no form or majesty that we should look at him, and no beauty that we should desire him. He was despised and rejected by men; a man of sorrows, and acquainted with grief; and as one from whom men hide their faces he was despised, and we esteemed him not. Surely he has borne our*

34. Matthew 2:23

35. John 1:46

36. Acts 24:5 For we have found this man a plague, one who stirs up riots among all the Jews throughout the world and is a ringleader of the sect of the Nazarenes.

> *griefs and carried our sorrows; yet we esteemed him stricken, smitten by God, and afflicted. But he was wounded for our transgressions; he was crushed for our iniquities; upon him was the chastisement that brought us peace, and with his stripes we are healed.*[37]

Jesus did not come establishing a Kingdom like the kings of the earth. He came associating himself with the despised, the rejected and the trampled. He came to undo the punishment and tears associated with sin. Until a person comes to the true King, he remains exiled from God. The only means by which you can avoid the judgment of God and be blessed is by being identified with a righteous King who will represent you in a New Covenant before God.

37. Isaiah 53:2-5

8 Not an Earthly Kingdom

The teachings of Jesus and John the Baptist highlight the fact that Jesus came to establish a Kingdom unlike the kingdoms of men. As we investigate what they taught about life in the Kingdom, we realize that God's intentions for us are far superior to the best ideas of men.

Preparing for the King

John the Baptist is one of the most significant characters in the book of Matthew. Unfortunately we often misunderstand him, his place, and his ministry. This error diminishes him in many minds. John came before Jesus, calling the people to repent[1] that they might be prepared for the coming Kingdom of God.[2] He came in fulfillment of the words of the prophet Isaiah:

> *A voice cries: "In the wilderness prepare the way of the Lord; make straight in the desert a highway for our God. Every valley shall be lifted up, and every mountain and hill be made low; the uneven ground shall become level, and the rough places a plain.*

---

1. Matthew 3

2. There is no difference between the Kingdom of God and the Kingdom of Heaven. Matthew followed the Jewish custom of using the word "God" sparingly, but even he used the two labels for the Kingdom interchangeably.

Matthew 19:23-24 And Jesus said to his disciples, "Truly, I say to you, only with difficulty will a rich person enter the *kingdom of heaven*. Again I tell you, it is easier for a camel to go through the eye of a needle than for a rich person to enter the *kingdom of God*." (emphasis added)

> *And the glory of the Lord shall be revealed, and all flesh shall see it together, for the mouth of the Lord has spoken."*[3]

John's purpose was to prepare the way for the Messiah. When a king was visiting, the route of his arrival was examined for obstacles, and anything that might hinder his approach was eliminated. The high spots in the road were removed and the holes were filled. We know the difference in driving over an old, rough road and the pleasure it is to drive on a freshly paved surface. It is so much better, quieter, and smoother. This was John's job.

However, it must be carefully noted that *John the Baptist did not have a shovel.* This reveals one of the most important aspects of the Kingdom of God: it is not an earthly kingdom. John prepared the hearts of people, not the roads of Judea. The place needing preparation is within the heart—your heart, my heart, and the hearts of all people. We are not called by God to build physical roads. We are called to smooth the way for the King to enter the hearts of men and women. We know that Jesus' Kingdom is not of this world because John the Baptist did not have a shovel.

Whenever we think God's Kingdom needs to be extended to make it an earthly kingdom, we have forgotten this very important lesson. Jesus did not come to establish an earthly kingdom, but a spiritual one. Everyone who follows him must first have his heart prepared by removing anything that hinders meeting the King. These are the spiritual issues of the heart, not the roads in an earthly kingdom.

The temptation of Christ

During his temptation by the devil in the wilderness,[4] Jesus emphasized important issues concerning the Kingdom, and his responses to temptation were established. The three temptations that Jesus faced represent the three forms of temptation we all face.

The first temptation of Jesus encompassed both his identity as Son of God and Son of Man. As Son of God, he had power to do as he pleased, including turning stones into bread. As Son of Man, he existed with all the physical appetites and bodily needs that you and I have. But Jesus chose to do the will of the Father rather than satisfy those appetites. He knew that *it is better to be good than to satisfy your*

3. Isaiah 40:3-5
4. Matthew 4

appetites.[5]

We have many different bodily appetites (e.g. hunger, thirst, sex), and we are tempted to exploit others in order to fulfill them. But living by appetite alone hinders your ability to obey God. Appetites are to be fulfilled in God's time and in God's way. Even if you have the power to fulfill them, it does not mean it is good for you to do so. Fulfilling appetites in a selfish way is relationally destructive.

The second temptation was for Jesus to make a spectacle of himself. The devil wanted Jesus to throw himself down from the temple in full view of everyone so that they would know who he was. In doing this, people would definitely follow Jesus, but for all the wrong reasons. Jesus knew that *it is better to be good than to have people like you.*

When you seek to look good in the eyes of others by having or doing that which makes people popular in this world, you adopt the value system of the world rather than God's value system. What people do to become popular rarely involves sacrificial love for the benefit of others. If Jesus had thrown himself off of the temple, it would have only gained a following for an earthly kingdom. So Jesus answered Satan with a verse implying that doing the wrong thing in order to look good before people removes us from the place of God's protection.[6]

The third temptation involved receiving an earthly kingdom rather than establishing a spiritual one through suffering. Jesus knew that *it is better to be good than to have an earthly kingdom.* People desire power and imagine the good they could do with it, but the quest for power often puts men under the devil and his authority.[7] Accepting an earthly kingdom would require Jesus to bow down before Satan at some level. However, Jesus' Kingdom was coming in order to free people from the devil's power and authority.

Jesus knew that it is better to be good than to have bodily appetites satisfied, to be popular, or to be powerful. Living for self tends to further corrupt our value systems and leads us away from God. The quest to satisfy self and gain attention and power flows from pride that has

5. Good, and how it relates to God, will be covered in Chapter 14: The Value System of the Kingdom.

6. Matthew 4:7 Jesus said to him, "Again it is written, 'You shall not put the Lord your God to the test.'"

7. Matthew 4:8-9 Again, the devil took him to a very high mountain and showed him all the kingdoms of the world and their glory. And he said to him, "All these I will give you, if you will fall down and worship me."

created a value system in opposition to God. We must be careful to know who we are listening to and in whose kingdom we truly are. It is better to be good, to be like God, and to have his value system than to satisfy our bodily appetites, to have people like us, and to have our own kingdoms with our own rules, power, and possessions.

The rules of the Kingdom

All kingdoms have laws for people to follow. Laws are the ethical system and the ideas of what is right and wrong by which a governed people are to live. The Jews had laws they followed, including the Ten Commandments, which were part of the Old Covenant.

Some claim Jesus made the laws more strict and insist the Old Testament Law still applies today, if only partially.[8] But we can see Jesus' Kingdom is different from the kingdom of Israel because of how he spoke of the Old Testament Law by which the people lived. Jesus said he fulfilled their Law.[9] Anyone who follows Jesus into his Kingdom no longer needs the Old Testament laws. The righteous standard of the Kingdom is our being as righteous as God,[10] which is a far higher standard than anyone lived by under the Law.

In the text commonly referred to as the Sermon on the Mount,[11] we have a collection of teachings Jesus gave on the value system of his Kingdom and how it differed from all earthly kingdoms. Here are a few elements from Jesus' teaching describing how he intended for those in his Kingdom to act toward each other.

Forgiveness rather than anger

The first law Jesus discussed was "You shall not murder."[12] Jesus made two points about how people must live in his Kingdom.[13] First,

---

8. Some suggest that the Mosaic Law can be broken into moral, legal, and ceremonial parts, not all of which were removed by Christ.

9. Matthew 5:17 Do not think that I have come to abolish the Law or the Prophets; I have not come to abolish them but to fulfill them.

10. See Appendix: Justification, Sanctification, and Glorification

11. Matthew 5-7

12. Matthew 5:21; Exodus 20:13

13. Matthew 5:22-24 But I say to you that everyone who is angry with his brother will be liable to judgment; whoever insults his brother will be liable to the council; and whoever says, 'You fool!' will be liable to the hell of fire. So if you are offering your gift at the altar and there remember that your brother has something against you, leave

you are not to be angry with another and call him nasty names like "fool." Second, you are to forgive those who have offended you, and ask those you have wronged to forgive you.

The Law prohibited murder, but Jesus taught that in his Kingdom you are not even to be angry with one another. Instead, you are to be forgiving. Jesus did not give the law "do not murder" in his Kingdom because he does not have an earthly, physical kingdom. In earthly, physical kingdoms someone must enforce all laws. But we do not enforce laws in Christianity like the governments of men do.

Jesus taught that you do not fit into his Kingdom simply by not murdering people. You fit into his Kingdom by not being angry with your brothers and sisters in the Kingdom. You fit into the Kingdom by forgiving and seeking forgiveness. Murder ultimately comes from unforgiveness, while love and forgiveness short-circuit the path to murder.

This is not a higher interpretation of the Law; it is a different ethical system. Since it is, the consequences for actions are not like those in an earthly kingdom. In Jesus' Kingdom, *the consequence of sin is forgiveness*, not anger, and relationship, not death.

Truth rather than oaths

Jesus then criticized the Jewish practice of promising to do something one did not intend to do.[14] Again, this is one of the Ten Commandments: "You shall not take the name of the Lord your God in vain."[15] Taking the Name of God in vain was making a promise using God's Name and then breaking that promise. By using replacements for God's Name, people created loopholes to break their promises if necessary. They swore an oath by the temple or the altar—promising, yet not technically using God's Name. It was a promise that could be broken without taking God's Name in vain, and a clever way of lying and doing evil while not breaking the letter of the Law.

But in Jesus' Kingdom, we must tell each other the truth. If we do, we need not ever add an oath to it. If you always tell the truth, you will never have to swear an oath that you are telling the truth. You do

---

your gift there before the altar and go. First be reconciled to your brother, and then come and offer your gift.

14. Matthew 5:33-37

15. Exodus 20:7

not fit into Jesus' Kingdom by keeping your oaths; you fit into Christ's Kingdom by always telling the truth.

However, we are still not fully at Jesus' point. Oaths are used in legal matters of the law. In Jesus' Kingdom there are no legal matters of the law that require oaths. Where there is no law, there is no legal system to enforce the law.

Jesus' Kingdom is not an earthly kingdom with earthly laws and legal proceedings. He requires we be completely open and honest and loving toward each other. The purpose of lying is to pretend to have one value system while holding another. Liars want the *benefits* of a common value system without actually *having* a common value system. But you can never truly be in Christ's Kingdom unless you share his value system.

Grace rather than laws

Jesus then spoke of the *lex talionis*, "an eye for an eye and a tooth for a tooth."[16] This method of justice sought to make everything even. If someone hurt another, the same injury was inflicted on the transgressor. No one should seek anything more from the offender; the just penalty was meted out, leaving no need for anything more to be done. Justice was considered fulfilled. Since the very nature of this is negative rather than positive, Jesus would not have it in his Kingdom.

When Jesus said, "If anyone slaps you on the right cheek, turn to him the other also,"[17] he was referring to an insult slap. To be struck on the right cheek presupposes that you are struck with the back of a person's hand since most people are right handed. Insults are not always physical; more often they are verbal. We tend to attack those who have attacked us, and strike as we have been struck.

Jesus mentioned three other issues as well: someone taking what is legally yours, being told to do something by one ruling over you, and having others pay you interest on a loan.[18] Jesus said for all these that *it is better to have a right heart than a legal right.* In the Kingdom of God, we must care more about people than about getting even with others or getting what belongs to us. In fact, in the Kingdom we go the extra mile even for those who rule over us because it is better to have a right

16. Leviticus 24:19-20 (cf. Deuteronomy 19:16-21; Exodus 21:22-25)

17. Matthew 5:39

18. Matthew 5:40-42

heart than a legal right.

In Christ's Kingdom, our concern for justice in our personal relationships should not be like people who live in earthly kingdoms. Where there is no earthly kingdom and accompanying law, there is no place to have your legal rights enforced. We are not under law, but grace. This is not a higher interpretation of the Law; it is a different ethical system.

Jesus commanded those in his Kingdom to respond with grace, even to those who offend and mistreat them. Justice in his Kingdom is not about getting even and making others suffer as you have, but about carrying a cross for those who have hurt us.

New consequences for sin

Jesus said he was the fulfillment or the perfection (completion) of the Old Testament Law.[19] The Old Testament Law only reveals some aspects of the value system of God. For example, by it we can learn how he considers human life to be valuable, that he keeps his promises so we need to keep ours, and that he is just.

The question you must face is this: Do you think God wanted people to live by "an eye for an eye and a tooth for a tooth"? Do you think God wanted people to only keep promises if they swore an oath using his Name? Do you think God wanted people to fight over who was right and who was wrong? Do you think God desires these laws for today, or for his Kingdom, or in any future Kingdom? Do these values reflect the true value system of God and Christ?

You must be careful how you answer those questions because it might betray how much you desire to live by the Law and not by the value system of the Kingdom of God. Your answers may reveal you desire your rights rather than love, mercy, and forgiveness. Even worse, your answers may reveal how confused you are about how the Old Covenant does not apply to Christ's Kingdom. It never has and it never will.

God allowed these laws as concessions because there is a problem inside the hearts of people.[20] Jesus' Kingdom is not one with rules

---

19. Matthew 5:17 Do not think that I have come to abolish the Law or the Prophets; I have not come to abolish them but to fulfill them.

Matthew 5:48 You therefore must be perfect, as your heavenly Father is perfect.

20. When Jesus spoke of divorce, he said Moses permitted it because of the hard-

that make people do the right thing through law and force. The laws of earthly, physical kingdoms are like that. Men use external means to compel people to act according to the laws of their kingdoms. But when we become what we ought to be internally, we do not need rules to make us act as we ought externally.

Jesus came to fix our hearts because if we become like him in loving others, we do not need rules to make us do good; we will love to do good to others. The Kingdom of God does not have these rules and they are not enforced as in the Old Testament or in any physical kingdom. Adherence to Christ's ethical system is the measure of the Kingdom and can only be enforced by loving those in the Kingdom. You are outside of the Kingdom if you persist in unloving actions toward others.[21]

Jesus did not make the Old Testament laws more strict. He taught that the fulfillment of them was *his* ethical system of sacrificial love for the benefit of others. This is greater than the ethical system of the Law.

Does the Old Testament Law still apply today?[22] No, because the higher ethical system of Jesus' Kingdom perfects and fulfills the lesser ethical system of the Law. The commandments are not relaxed; they are triumphed over by love and mercy.[23]

In Christ's Kingdom, the consequence for sinning against someone is not "an eye for an eye." Instead, it is receiving love and forgiveness. Jesus' Kingdom operates alongside earthly kingdoms; but when we live his ethical system, the values of his Kingdom bleed over into the earthly kingdoms in which we reside.

Being good, not just looking good

People do good deeds for different reasons. Some do good because they are good. Some do good because they are afraid of getting caught doing evil. And some do good because they want people to

---

ness of people's hearts (Matthew 19:8). The Law did not perfectly reveal the value system of God, and it did not supply the means to keep it.

21. Church discipline only confirms the reality of a person's distance from God. When a professing believer persists in sin, his removal from the fellowship is an earthly demonstration of his separation from God (cf. Matthew 18:15-20; 1 Corinthians 5).

22. Matthew 5:19 Therefore whoever relaxes one of the least of these commandments and teaches others to do the same will be called least in the kingdom of heaven, but whoever does them and teaches them will be called great in the kingdom of heaven.

23. James 2:13

think they are good, even if they are not. In earthly kingdoms there is always status to be gained through doing actions that impress others. But in the Kingdom of God, you do not have to try to impress anyone.

Jesus addressed three deeds the Jews believed could measure the goodness of a person: giving to the poor, praying, and fasting.[24] Giving to the poor and needy, praying to God, and fasting (going without food or other needs as a sign of contrition) can all be good deeds. What, then, was Jesus criticizing?

In each of these situations the people were doing good acts only so others would *think* they were good, not because they actually *were* good. They wanted people to think they were in God's Kingdom, but they did not really want to *be* in his Kingdom and adopt his value system. By using the wrong standard, people can be deceived as to who is in the Kingdom of God.

Giving to the poor does not make you part of the Kingdom of God. Someone who is in the Kingdom will do this, but this is not how you get into the Kingdom. Praying does not make you part of the Kingdom. Someone who is in the Kingdom will pray, but this is not how you get into the Kingdom. Fasting can be beneficial, and someone who is in the Kingdom may fast, but fasting is not how you get into the Kingdom.

Jesus warned against doing anything only to make others think you were in his Kingdom. He taught that *it is better to be good than to have people think you are good.* God does good to us because he is good. He also wants us to be good—not merely doers of good deeds.

What is the difference? If your heart is good like God's, you will desire to do what is good to others. If you are not good, then you only do good deeds because you want people to think you are something you are not, or because you are afraid of being caught doing the evil deeds you really desire. Being good is far more important than appearing good. It reveals that you are gloriously transformed in your heart, and not merely reflecting God's glory by keeping rules.

Forgiveness in the Kingdom

Jesus then taught his disciples how they should pray. Unsurprisingly, the Lord's Prayer is all about the King and his Kingdom. Heaven is heaven because God's will, his value system, is perfectly done there.

24. Matthew 6:1-34

We experience his Kingdom here on earth when we live his value system in our relationships.

> *Pray then like this: "Our Father in heaven, hallowed be your name. Your kingdom come, your will be done, on earth as it is in heaven. Give us this day our daily bread, and forgive us our debts, as we also have forgiven our debtors. And lead us not into temptation, but deliver us from evil. For if you forgive others their trespasses, your heavenly Father will also forgive you, but if you do not forgive others their trespasses, neither will your Father forgive your trespasses."*[25]

Most people do not have access to the king, president, or prime minister of the country in which they live; but we have an audience with our King any time we want. In earthly kingdoms, people have to do something special to be noticed by the king; but we do not have to be outstanding in order for Christ to invite us to come before him. In God's Kingdom we do not have to do good deeds to make him think we are good. He already knows if we are trying to be good or not. You cannot fool him into thinking you are good when you are only pretending.

God does not want you to do good deeds to make him happy with you. He wants you to do good to others because you are good and because you want to be like him. The most important way in which God wants us to be like him is in forgiving one another. The forgiveness we seek is tied to the kind of forgivers we ourselves are: "forgive us our debts, as we also have forgiven our debtors." This is a staggering flaw in most people's understanding of God's forgiveness. *He ties our forgiveness from him to the degree we are like him.* Foremost in his value system is forgiveness, because God's value system most looks like Jesus on the cross. Unless we forgive as he does, we will not be forgiven by him.

Jesus encouraged his disciples to keep their relationships with one another strong by dealing with sin and conflicts.[26] When someone sins, the people involved need to talk about it and seek to resolve the problem. This teaching prompted Peter to ask how many times he must forgive someone. Like Peter, we all know the frustration of dealing with people who continue to hurt us, and how we are tempted to give up on them.

---

25. Matthew 6:9-15

26. Matthew 18:15-20

Jesus told Peter that his Kingdom was like a king who wanted to settle accounts with his servants.[27] One of the men in the kingdom owed a great sum of money to the king, far more than he could repay. The king ordered that all the man had, including his wife and children, be sold in order to settle the debt. The man fell on his knees, begging the king to give him time, promising to repay everything. The king had pity on the man, deciding instead to forgive his entire debt. He was free to go.

Leaving the presence of the king, he found another man indebted to him. Receiving a request for mercy similar to his own, he responded with hardness and had the man thrown in prison until the debt was repaid. When the king learned of this, he was outraged. He called the wicked man before him and had him thrown in prison, reinstating his impossible debt. The king overturned his previous ruling because of the man's refusal to be forgiving to others as the king had been to him.

Forgiveness is so important to God because it is the cornerstone of his value system. If God's value system most looks like Jesus dying on the cross, then we are most like God when we forgive. More than anything else, unforgiveness reveals that we do not have his value system and are not in his Kingdom. Forgiving one another is something God takes very seriously. We cannot be like him and remain unforgiving. The worst offense done to us is minor compared to the great offense we have done to God. Anyone who appreciates God's forgiveness will demonstrate it by forgiving others.

After teaching the disciples about prayer and forgiveness, Jesus continued to elaborate that theme.[28] God has only two ways of dealing with us: mercy or judgment. The method we use with others will be the method used with us. When tempted to judge another person, we must judge with the same standard by which we desire to be judged. If we want to be treated mercifully when we sin, we must be merciful to others when they sin. It is perfectly acceptable to evaluate the lives of others and seek to help them change. Each time we condemn others we are not helping them. We are demonstrating how we are sinfully unaware of our own failures and our own need of mercy from God.

Jesus' point is clear: if we seek forgiveness from God, we will certainly receive it. But what we seek from him, we must also offer to

27. Matthew 18:21-35

28. Matthew 7 has one theme: We must adopt God's value system of forgiveness.

others. If we wish to be forgiven, then we must be forgivers. If we seek good gifts from our God, we must be givers of good gifts ourselves.[29]

Jesus warned against false teachers who would come and even work miracles.[30] In spite of the wonders they performed, they could be recognized as false if they did not have sacrificial love for others. The absence of mercy reveals that a person is not truly in Christ's Kingdom, for his Kingdom is the place where mercy is most plentiful. In order to enter his Kingdom, we must do what he says. We must adopt his value system of forgiveness, mercy, and sacrificial love.

Jesus' Kingdom is not an earthly kingdom. The standard by which you are called to live in the Kingdom is far higher than the laws of any earthly kingdom. You cannot fake whether or not you are in it. To receive the benefits of the Kingdom, you must live by the rules of the Kingdom. You must spiritually change, having your heart transformed to Christ-likeness.

29. Matthew 7:7-12

30. Matthew 7:15-27

9 The Authority of the King

Jesus proclaimed the Gospel in terms of his Kingdom. Acceptance of the King and his divine authority is the first step in understanding all that Jesus taught. In the Kingdom of God, there is no higher authority than Christ. Anyone wishing to enter the Kingdom must recognize Jesus' authority and submit to it. There are several aspects to his authority that we must understand as we come to him.

Faith recognizes Jesus' authority is from God

Once, when entering Capernaum, Jesus met a Roman soldier whose servant was seriously ill.[1] The centurion approached Jesus, requesting healing for his servant. Jesus offered to go to the man's home and heal the servant, but the centurion replied, "Lord, I am not worthy to have you come under my roof, but only say the word, and my servant will be healed." The man understood that even as he had authority to direct his men to go and act for him, so also Jesus had authority to speak and have his will be done. Jesus then spoke to the crowd standing around, "Truly, I tell you, with no one in Israel have I found such faith."

Since Jesus marveled at the man's faith, it is important to discover exactly what the centurion believed about Jesus. Although he believed Jesus could heal from a distance, this was not what amazed Jesus. The central issue was his recognition that Jesus was from God. Jesus need-

1. Matthew 8:5-13

ed only to speak because God gave him authority.

The centurion was able to grasp this since he was accustomed to having his men obey him when he gave instructions. They obeyed him because he derived his authority from Caesar. If they disobeyed their commander, they were really disobeying Caesar. If they disobeyed their commander, they would answer to Caesar. Ultimately, all power and authority in Caesar's kingdom flowed down from him to others.

The centurion believed that if Jesus really were from God, then all he needed to do was speak the word and God would make it happen. Whoever disobeyed Jesus would answer to God. Recognizing the source of Jesus' authority caused the man to regard himself as unworthy to have Jesus enter his house.

We learn another very important thing about Christ's Kingdom from this story as well. His Kingdom is not only for Jews, but for all people of the world. In fact, some Gentiles enter it while some Jews do not. What makes the difference? Only those who recognize that Jesus' authority comes from God may enter the Kingdom of God, and no one can enter the Kingdom of God without recognizing Jesus' authority in his Kingdom. Faith is important because Jesus' Kingdom is not an earthly kingdom. You cannot see it; you can only enter it by faith that Jesus is from God.

We must have faith in Jesus' authority

Later, Jesus and his disciples were caught in a storm at sea.[2] Jesus slept while the men struggled against the wind and waves, fearful they would perish in the storm. When they finally woke Jesus, he rebuked the storm; but he also rebuked the disciples for their lack of faith.

His disciples were afraid because they did not have faith. Fear and faith cannot occupy the same space. Fear drives out faith, and faith drives out fear. When they had one, they could not have the other. Their fear of the storm revealed their lack of faith; but a lack of faith in what?

First, it showed a lack of confidence in Jesus' mission and God's promised fulfillment of that mission. If they had faith, they would know that God would protect them and that Jesus' mission would not come to an end because of a storm. Second, they did not believe Jesus' most recent instructions. He told his disciples, "Let us cross over to the

2. Matthew 8:23-27

other side of the lake."[3] If Jesus said they would do something, then surely they would do it. To entertain the idea that Jesus' plan could be thwarted by a storm reveals a lack of faith in his authority that proceeded from the God who parted the Red Sea.

Faith is believing the promises of God. This means not merely believing he *can* do what he has said, but believing that he *will* do what he has promised. When we believe that Jesus will do as he promised, it is faith in his God-derived authority.

Jesus' authority reveals value systems

These stories of faith and Jesus' authority are followed by two more stories demonstrating his authority. The first concerns his authority over the spirit world, and the second his authority to forgive sins.

Jesus entered a Gentile region where men were raising pigs.[4] There were two demon-possessed men living in the tombs nearby, and Jesus cast the demons from the men into the pigs. The men were saved, but the pigs were lost since they ran into the sea and drowned.

When the people of the area heard of this, they asked Jesus to leave because they were not ready to enter his Kingdom. They were Gentiles, not Jews, and did not have the faith to understand his authority. Remember, the value system of Jesus' Kingdom is sacrificial love for the benefit of others. These people were more concerned about pigs than people. That is precisely why Jesus let the pigs die: to reveal the value system of the people.

Any time we allow our business and financial interests to take precedence over the care and well-being of others, we give pigs the priority. We share the value system of these people in the story rather than sharing the value system of Christ. He allowed the business to die in order to reveal the heart of the community.

Jesus has authority to forgive sins

Traveling back to his home city, Jesus demonstrated his authority to forgive sins.[5] Some people brought to Jesus a paralyzed man, to whom he said, "Your sins are forgiven." The scribes who were present believed Jesus was blaspheming since only God could forgive sins.

---

3. Mark 4:35
4. Matthew 8:28-34
5. Matthew 9:1-8

Jesus challenged their thinking by demonstrating that his authority to forgive sins came from the same source as his ability to heal the man. He asked them if it were easier to say, "Your sins are forgiven" or to say, "Rise and walk." Of course, saying something and having it happen are two different things. If one can actually do what one says, then it is true.

Jesus did what the scribes thought was easier; he healed a man. He did this to prove he had the authority to forgive sins—the other work of God. How did the man know his sins were forgiven? By faith. He believed the words Jesus said. The miracle helped him believe, but he still put his trust in the words of Christ for what he could not see.

Here we learn another lesson about the Kingdom: Jesus has authority to forgive sins. This is why the man who believed could also be forgiven. The faith that enabled him to believe Jesus could heal him led to faith that Jesus could also forgive him. Never forget that forgiveness is greater than physical healing, and that transformation of value system is more miraculous than any sign or wonder.

The once-lame man entered the Kingdom of Christ and was forgiven, but the Pharisees did not enter the Kingdom because they did not believe Jesus could forgive sins. Both saw the miracle, but only one had faith. The crucial point about the Kingdom in this story is that only those who believe Jesus can forgive their sins may enter the Kingdom.

The one rule of the Kingdom

Jesus invited his followers to come to him and receive rest.[6] Is your life with God a burden? According to Jesus it should not be.

To understand "rest" we must understand laws and the Sabbath. Imagine having rules regarding which foods you could and could not eat, and rules mandating which activities you could not do on certain days. These are not necessarily bad; after all, everyone has to follow rules. However, keeping religious rules such as these may not even be worship.

The Sabbath was a day set aside for the Jews to remember both

6. Matthew 11:28-30 "Come to me, all who labor and are heavy laden, and I will give you rest. Take my yoke upon you, and learn from me, for I am gentle and lowly in heart, and you will find rest for your souls. For my yoke is easy, and my burden is light."

God's work and his rest. Some took great joy in it, while others considered it a very serious day. They believed that if they could do everything in the Law perfectly, following all the rules, God would bless them. Therefore, they made up new rules to keep from accidently breaking the Law. Their thinking was something like this: If it is wrong to work on the Sabbath, we need a rule to make writing on the Sabbath wrong. And if it is wrong to write on the Sabbath, we need a rule to make it wrong to even touch a pen on the Sabbath.

In all of this, they completely missed the point of the Sabbath. The purpose of a day of rest was for the people to rest from their labor. If God mandated rest, people could not exploit others by requiring them to work seven days a week. The Sabbath day was intended by God to ensure people were not exploited, and to give an opportunity to reflect on God's goodness to them.

We receive Jesus' rest by doing his value system of sacrificial love for others. We need not be bothered by lists of rules and laws, desperately trying to please him. If we love others, and do not exploit them, we are doing the value system of the Kingdom. This one rule of love captures all that God values and requires of us.

Jesus makes the rules in his Kingdom

With this view of the Sabbath, we are prepared to understand another Sabbath story in which Jesus and his disciples were walking through grain fields. Becoming hungry, they picked a few heads of grain and began eating them.[7] According to the Pharisees, they were reaping, and it was not lawful to harvest grain on the Sabbath. Although reaping was considered work, Jesus' disciples were merely snacking to satisfy their hunger. It is the same as when you pick berries as you walk along a trail. Your intention is not to pick buckets full to preserve or sell, but only a few to enjoy for the moment.

However, the Pharisees said it was wrong. When confronted about the behavior of his disciples, Jesus did not answer directly, but told them a story from the life of David. While on the run from the murderous King Saul, David received from some priests bread that, according to the Law, only priests were allowed to eat. He was hungry and needy, and the priests freely gave him the bread. Furthermore, God never condemned David for eating the special bread.

---

7. Matthew 12:1-8

David was given the bread out of love and because he was in need. If, under those circumstances, David was permitted to do something the Law forbade, how could the Pharisees condemn an action neither mentioned in the Law, nor hurtful to anyone? How could they condemn picking grain for a snack?

Jesus also made another point. Priests *were* permitted to work on the Sabbath because they were obeying the rules of God for the temple; they were protected by his authority. Similarly, Jesus was free to make the rules for those in his Kingdom. If he did not condemn his disciples, neither could the Pharisees. They were protected because they were in his Kingdom and lived by the rules of their King.

In the Kingdom, mercy is more important than strictly following ceremonial laws.[8] Mercy is the action commanded by Christ for all those in his Kingdom. When we are under his rule and authority and live by his value system, we are no longer obligated to follow any other religious traditions.

It is never wrong to do good

Jesus had one more lesson for the Jews regarding his authority, his value system, and the Sabbath. He entered a synagogue where there was a man suffering with a withered hand.[9] Seeking to trap him, the Pharisees asked, "Is it lawful to heal on the Sabbath?" They wanted to know if Jesus would heal the man's hand on the holy day.

Jesus set the stage for his response by asking them a rhetorical question about their ethical system. If they considered it permissible on the Sabbath to rescue an animal whose life was in danger, then could he heal a man who was worth much more than an animal?

The problem the Pharisees had with the equation was that the man's life was not in danger. They had various rules regarding what could be done for a sick person on the Sabbath. A person could be helped, but work needed to be avoided in the process of helping or healing. So Jesus made it a question of what is good: "Is it lawful to do good on the Sabbath?" Can you ever place any limits on doing good? Does doing good break the Sabbath?

Then Jesus healed the man, while the Pharisees condemned him

8. Jesus also permanently removed the need for any animal sacrifices in his Kingdom.

9. Matthew 12:9-14

as a sinner for breaking the Sabbath. Jesus *did good,* but the Pharisees, who were so concerned about pleasing God, *did evil*—on the Sabbath—by condemning Jesus as a sinner.

This is really an issue of dominion. In Jesus' Kingdom it is always lawful to do good no matter what day it is. Not only is it lawful, it is a requirement in the Kingdom. The Pharisees' problem derived from the fact that they were not in Christ's Kingdom, and they did not accept the rule he made for his Kingdom. They lived outside the Kingdom and held a different value system.

The value system of the Kingdom of God is sacrificial love for the benefit of others. It is not burdensome. It is not a confusing list of rules and laws. There is only one easy thing to remember; one idea simple enough for a child to understand. The most beautiful part of the Kingdom is that the King treats all those in his Kingdom with sacrificial love for their benefit. He does not ask you to have sacrificial love without also being a sacrificial lover. Jesus makes the rules for his Kingdom, and they apply equally to all those in his Kingdom.

10 Faith and Sacrificial Love

The story of Jesus feeding the five thousand occurs in all four Gospel accounts, marking its importance. In Matthew's account of the story,[1] the stage is set by first mentioning Herod's murder of John the Baptist. When John spoke against Herod's sin, Herod killed John because he erroneously believed John was trying to stir the people up against him politically.[2]

When Jesus learned of the death of John, he desired solitude. This seems to be a very normal reaction to such sad news since John was more than a friend—he was Jesus' relative. John's murder may also have sparked in Jesus thoughts of his own impending death on the cross. So, Jesus took a boat ride in order to find a desolate place to be alone.

However, Jesus could not escape the people who followed him. Not only was he facing many internal feelings because of John's death, he now had to deal with a potentially dangerous crowd. In the Gospel of John, we learn that they wanted to make Jesus king[3]—a sentiment

1. Matthew 14

2. Herod divorced his first wife, causing a political problem because she was a neighboring king's daughter. When Herod subsequently married his half-brother's wife, John denounced the immoral union. Though speaking to the moral situation, Herod thought John agitated the political one as well, especially since John was preaching about the coming Messianic Kingdom.

3. John 6:15 Perceiving then that they were about to come and take him by force to make him king, Jesus withdrew again to the mountain by himself.

that might stir Herod to murderous anger against Jesus. In the same circumstances, I might feel like asking the people to leave me alone for a while; but rather than thinking of himself, Jesus thought of the people. He went ashore and healed their sick. Loving like Jesus requires loving others even when we are hurting.

That evening, the disciples asked Jesus to send the people away to buy food for themselves, but Jesus said they did not need to go. Instead, he instructed his disciples to give them something to eat. Some understand this to mean that Jesus expected the disciples to teach the people; but, since Jesus ultimately fed them food, he obviously expected the disciples to actually feed them.

Jesus would never ask his disciples to do something they did not have the means to do. Since there was only a small amount of food available—five small loaves and two fish—their other option was to spend a large sum of money purchasing food for the crowd. The disciples possessed the finances, but could not imagine parting with them.[4] It would have been very costly for them to purchase that much food; it would have been a great sacrifice.

Here we learn one of the greatest lessons of the Kingdom. Sacrificial love takes great faith that God will provide. When the most that the disciples would contribute was five loaves and two fish,[5] Jesus blessed the meager meal and had his disciples distribute it to the people. Thousands ate from the initially small meal. Jesus miraculously provided bread in the wilderness even as God had done during the

---

4. Some interpreters believe that Jesus' command to feed the multitude was only to ensure that his disciples knew there were no means available other than the miraculous. They also presuppose that Jesus and his disciples could not have possessed the necessary money (see Appendix: Jesus' Finances). However, the biblical texts clearly contain Christ's command for his disciples to feed the multitude, and also indicate both their ability and their reluctance to obey. Jesus' ultimate miraculous feeding of the people does not negate what the disciples could have done.

Mark 6:37 But he answered them, "You give them something to eat." And they said to him, "Shall we go and buy two hundred denarii worth of bread and give it to them to eat?"

Luke 9:13 But he said to them, "You give them something to eat." They said, "We have no more than five loaves and two fish—unless we are to go and buy food for all these people."

John 6:5-6 Lifting up his eyes, then, and seeing that a large crowd was coming toward him, Jesus said to Philip, "Where are we to buy bread, so that these people may eat?" He said this to test him, for he himself knew what he would do.

5. Even the little they did offer was given by a child (John 6:9).

Exodus. This was a sign of who he was and why he had come.

Jesus, still desiring to be alone, sent his disciples ahead of him by boat. It seems safe to presume that Jesus instructed them to meet him somewhere later; and if he failed to arrive by a certain time, to go on ahead without him. Jesus dismissed the crowd and then went away to pray by himself. He finally got what he wanted and needed: time alone with his Father.

Meanwhile, the disciples were out on the water, far from shore, with the wind and waves battering against them. In the darkness of night they saw something coming toward them over the water. They were very afraid, thinking they saw a ghost or spirit. They cried out in fear, probably asking God to protect them from a demon. "God save us! Help us!" they shouted. But it was Jesus walking on the water, and he called out to them, "It's me, don't be afraid!"

Now the story takes a very unexpected turn. Peter called out, "Lord, if it is you, command me to come to you on the water." What Peter asked is fascinating. Why would he ask that? Perhaps it was to test if what he saw was real. I think Peter was trying to determine if Jesus was miraculously overpowering nature. Jesus might merely be tricking the disciples, but by experiencing it for himself, Peter could verify its reality. Peter's request was really about the identity of Jesus. He wanted to determine the *nature* of who Jesus was, not merely the *identity* of who was walking on water.

Jesus told Peter to come to him, and Peter walked to Jesus on the surface of the water. But when Peter's attention shifted to the wind, he became afraid and cried out, "Lord save me!" Of course, Jesus took his hand and rescued him, but he also said, "O you of little faith, why did you doubt?" Once Jesus entered the boat, the wind stopped and the disciples exclaimed, "Truly you are the Son of God!"

The crucial part of this story is Jesus' remark to Peter about having little faith. Faith is what allows us to walk where Jesus walked. Peter's faith allowed him to walk as Jesus, but only while he had faith. Once his faith faded, so did his ability *because the power was not his own.*

What do we learn about faith and sacrificial love from this story? The disciples chose not to feed the crowd from their own provisions. Sacrificial love for others is costly and difficult. It is only possible by being unselfish and being willing to give. Sacrificial love for the benefit of others is only possible through faith in Christ.

Faith in Christ allows us to do what he did, especially when he took up the cross. We might be afraid of the dangers of loving like Jesus, and those fears will take away our ability to love like Jesus. The power to love sacrificially is not our own; it comes from the one who has power over nature.

Our nature is to be selfish and self-protective, and that is not the value system of the Kingdom. In order to live the value system of the Kingdom, we must have faith that Jesus will protect us and care for us when we sacrifice. We must believe that we will have food to eat when we give ours away, and that he will take our hand when we attempt the impossible. And we must believe he has enough power over nature to change our nature.

Sacrificial love takes great faith. Sacrificial love for the benefit of others—loving like Jesus all the time—is *as difficult as walking on water.* The miracle of feeding is tied to the disciples' unwillingness to provide for the crowd through their own resources. And it is also tied to the idea that faith is necessary to walk where Jesus walks. We must have faith in Christ in order to love sacrificially as he does.

Herod, who killed John the Baptist, heard about Jesus and thought he was John raised from the dead. Of course he was not John, but one day Jesus would indeed be raised from the dead. These miracles are important because they show Jesus' power and authority over nature. He did miracles that reminded the people of what God did in the Old Testament: feeding a multitude in the wilderness and controlling the waters of the Red Sea and the Jordan. Jesus is King of the Kingdom of God, and his Kingdom is the fulfillment of the promises of God in the Old Testament.

The feeding story and the walking on the water story form one unit. They both describe Jesus' power over nature, not only over the physical world, but also over the nature of our hearts. Sacrificial love for the benefit of others takes great faith that God will provide for you even when you sacrifice. It takes faith to walk where Jesus walked: You can only walk in sacrificial love by his power; and only while believing in his ability and not your own. Sacrificial love for the benefit of others is miraculous because it is as difficult for us to do as walking on water.

11 A Kingdom for Everyone

To avoid constant disruption from the crowds, Jesus took his disciples away for some rest and relaxation.[1] They travelled to the region of Tyre and Sidon, a Gentile territory north of Judea. There they met a Canaanite woman who cried out to Jesus, "Have mercy on me, O Lord, Son of David; my daughter is severely oppressed by a demon." The interesting thing about her request was her use of Jesus' kingly title, "Son of David."

This mother was very persistent in asking for help. Her desperation refused to allow her to leave without resolving her daughter's problem. But she began to get on the disciples' nerves. They asked Jesus to grant her request, if for no other reason than that she might leave them in peace. Jesus, however, told his disciples that he was sent only to the lost sheep of the house of Israel.

Jesus had healed other Gentiles before, but was reluctant to do so on this occasion. We need to understand what was different this time. In his other contacts with Gentiles, Jesus had been in the Israelite homeland. Furthermore, he had not gone to this Gentile area to heal and minister, but to rest. He did not travel there to seek the lost, but to train his disciples. If he began healing, the crowds would soon overwhelm them and disrupt their time together.

Even if this woman used the name "Son of David," it did not mean she was entitled to have whatever she asked. All requests to Jesus still

1. Matthew 15:21-28

had to relate to his Kingdom. If all she wanted was a miracle and not the King, he would not help her.

Seeing that Jesus continued to refuse her despite the disciples' urging, she knelt before him and pleaded, "Help me!" Jesus finally answered her, "It is not right to take the children's bread and throw it to the dogs." Ouch! Although that sounds harsh to us, the time Jesus was spending with the disciples was precious. They were the children and they needed his attention. To take it from them would be like giving children's food to dogs.

Jesus' use of children and dogs focused the woman's attention on the distinction between Jew and Gentile. Did she really understand the difference? Did she know her history? She answered, "Yes, Lord, yet even the dogs eat the crumbs that fall from their master's table."

What she was really saying was, "Yes, I may be a dog to a Jew or compared to your disciples. My needs may not be worse than everyone else's. And yes, the King was promised to the Jews. But even if I cannot sit at the table, I can at least have some crumbs off the floor."

She did understand her history! The Jewish prophets had spoken to the Gentiles in the Old Testament. They told the Gentiles to repent, and they promised that one day even the Gentiles could receive the Messiah when he came. Even if his Kingdom had not yet come to all nations, it did not reduce the fact that it *was* for all nations and not only for Jews. She had faith in a Messiah who would bless even her.

Her answer even suggested that the meal they were currently eating did not have to be interrupted for her daughter to be healed. Jesus did not have to leave his disciples; he could do it and never leave the table. It was as simple as brushing crumbs down for a dog.

What do we learn about the Kingdom? We learn that it is for all people who will come to it. It is not only for Jews, but for all the people of the whole world. But in order to enter it, they must acknowledge who the King is; that he truly is the Son of David. The woman had true faith, so Jesus provided the healing she sought for her daughter. Her faith was in a King for all nations and all peoples. She was not merely using his title to exploit him; she really believed in who he was.

After this, Jesus returned to the place where he had previously cast the demons into the pigs. Previously, the people sent him away, but now as he returned, they came to ask for healings while praising the

God of Israel.[2] Remember, these people were Gentiles.

The crowd stayed with Jesus for three days. Although in need of food, they did not want to leave him. Jesus asked his disciples what should be done for them. This time the disciples did not speak of the cost in feeding the multitude, but only of the availability of purchasing food in such a desolate place.[3] Perhaps they were now willing to sacrifice their money if only a supply could be found.

Why did they not ask Jesus for a miraculous multiplication of food? Surely they had not forgotten how Jesus fed the five thousand. Perhaps they did not suggest a miracle since the earlier crowd of Jews was rebuked for merely wanting bread and not wanting all of Jesus' teaching.[4] Or, more likely, they did not ask for a miraculous feeding since the people were Gentiles and not Jews, the children of Israel.

But Jesus did feed them miraculously. He fed a crowd of four thousand people with only seven loaves and a few fish. Afterward, they picked up seven basketfuls of leftovers. The beautiful truth about the Kingdom is that Jesus offers the Gentiles more than crumbs under the table. He offers them a full table in the wilderness prepared for them by God. Once they became willing to receive him as the King of the Kingdom of God, they could freely join him at his table.

---

2. Matthew 15:29-39

3. Matthew 15:33 And the disciples said to him, "Where are we to get enough bread in such a desolate place to feed so great a crowd?"

4. John 6:26 Jesus answered them, "Truly, truly, I say to you, you are seeking me, not because you saw signs, but because you ate your fill of the loaves."

12 The Keys to the Kingdom

One day, the Pharisees asked Jesus for a sign to prove who he was.[1] Jesus told them the reason they asked him for a sign was because they did not understand the signs and times as well as they thought they did. Then Jesus told them that the definitive sign given to them would be the sign of Jonah.

Jonah was swallowed by a great fish and kept in its belly for three days.[2] After that time, the fish spat Jonah out.[3] By mentioning Jonah, Jesus indicated that the sign of death and resurrection would be given to the Jewish leaders.[4] People often ask how a person could survive three days inside the belly of a fish. The answer is simple: they cannot—unless God does something. Likewise, people do not rise from the dead—unless God does something.

Jesus warned his disciples against the attitude of the Sadducees

---

1. Matthew 16
2. Jonah 1:17
3. Jonah 2:10
4. Matthew 12:38-41 Then some of the scribes and Pharisees answered him, saying, "Teacher, we wish to see a sign from you." But he answered them, "An evil and adulterous generation seeks for a sign, but no sign will be given to it except the sign of the prophet Jonah. For just as Jonah was three days and three nights in the belly of the great fish, so will the Son of Man be three days and three nights in the heart of the earth. The men of Nineveh will rise up at the judgment with this generation and condemn it, for they repented at the preaching of Jonah, and behold, something greater than Jonah is here."

and the Pharisees. Though they saw the signs proving who Jesus was, they still wanted a messiah on their own terms. The Pharisees wanted a messiah according to their own ideas of what he should be, while the Sadducees did not believe in either a messiah or a resurrection. Jesus taught his disciples that rejecting the Messiah because he does not meet your own expectations was the leaven of the Pharisees.

Next, Jesus asked his disciples who people said he was. Their answers included John the Baptist, Elijah, Jeremiah, or some other prophet. Then the crucial question followed: "Who do you say that I am?" Peter answered astutely, "You are the Christ, the Son of the living God."[5] For this response, Jesus stated that Peter held the keys to the Kingdom.

Keys are for gaining access to something. Keys to the Kingdom are about gaining access to the Kingdom of God. How do you get into the Kingdom? By knowing who the King is. The key to the Kingdom is fully knowing who Jesus is.

How does someone know who Jesus is? Not by signs, for the Pharisees saw signs and were not convinced. Jesus said the only way someone can know Jesus' true identity is by revelation from God the Father.[6] But knowing that Jesus is the Christ is only the beginning.

Jesus warned his disciples to refrain from telling anyone he was the Christ. There was a very simple reason for this prohibition: the disciples did not yet know enough to start telling others who Jesus was. Their understanding of the Messiah was incomplete. They knew the "Who" but they did not yet know the "why."

Their understanding of the Messiah still lacked a proper faith in *what kind* of Messiah he truly was. Jesus told them he would suffer, die, and be resurrected: the sign of Jonah![7] Yet that was a very difficult thing to believe. It was so difficult that even Peter, who believed Jesus was the Christ, was himself not yet able to accept a dying Messiah—the very leaven of the Pharisees Jesus warned them about.

Peter even promised he would fight to ensure that Jesus would not suffer or die. Jesus responded to him by saying, "Get behind me, Satan!" The words of Peter were not the values of God, but of man and

5. Matthew 16:16

6. Matthew 16:17 And Jesus answered him, "Blessed are you, Simon Bar-Jonah! For flesh and blood has not revealed this to you, but my Father who is in heaven."

7. Matthew 16:21-23

Satan. Remember Jesus' temptation at the beginning of his ministry?[8] There is no earthly kingdom of God, but there is a suffering Messiah. These two ideas were both very difficult to accept.

Jesus' death on the cross forms the basis of the Kingdom; without it there is no key to entering it. The value system of the Kingdom is sacrificial love for the benefit of others. Without the cross, there could be no Kingdom. Without the cross, there is no Gospel and no good news of the Kingdom of God.

The keys of the Kingdom are a true knowledge of the Messiah: that his Kingdom is not earthly but spiritual, and that the King must die a sacrificial death. The cross provides redemption and reconciliation, and it is the only means to restored relationship with God. But the cross also provides the example of God's love. We cannot fully know the depths of sacrificial love without first seeing God die on the cross for our sins.

Jesus stated very clearly what he expected of his disciples: they should become like him on the cross.

> *If anyone would come after me, let him deny himself and take up his cross and follow me. For whoever would save his life will lose it, but whoever loses his life for my sake will find it. For what will it profit a man if he gains the whole world and forfeits his life? Or what shall a man give in return for his life?*[9]

Sacrificial love is the rule of the Kingdom. You have two options: follow Christ in sacrificial love by loving like Christ on the cross, or have for yourself an earthly kingdom. Following Christ requires you to take up a cross and lose your life for God and others. The other option is you fighting for your life and seeking to gain as much of this world in the process.

You can be in God's Kingdom or you can be in your own kingdom, but you cannot be in both. In Christ's Kingdom you lose yourself for the sake of others. In your own kingdom you get what you want now, but lose your soul in the process. One leads to life, peace, and heaven; the other leads to death.

Carrying a cross—losing your life for the sake of others—requires faith that God keeps his promises. We need great faith to follow Jesus'

---

8. Matthew 4 (see Chapter 8: Not an Earthly Kingdom)
9. Matthew 16:24-26

footsteps to the cross, because sacrificial love for the benefit of others is as difficult as walking on water. You cannot do it without the power of God.

To enter the Kingdom, you must know that Jesus is the King of God's Kingdom. You must choose to follow Jesus as he has revealed himself, and not according to your preconceived ideas of who he is and what he must do. His spiritual Kingdom stands opposed to all the kingdoms of this earth, beginning with the smallest of your own making.

13 Faith Moves Mountains

Before Herod murdered John the Baptist, he imprisoned him.[1] John was demoralized, even as Elijah had been when he fled to Mount Horeb.[2] Some would argue that John had good reason to be discouraged. He was in prison and it seemed as though the message he preached of imminent blessing and judgment was taking a long time to be fulfilled. John did not understand how this was working out; if the Messiah was here, why was he in prison?[3]

Therefore, John sent his disciples to ask Jesus, "Are you the one who is to come, or shall we look for another?" In response, Jesus quoted the Old Testament book of Isaiah.[4] He told John's disciples to return and tell John that the blessings were here in the miracles, healings and the preaching of the Kingdom. However, Jesus was not prepared to quote the judgment portions of Isaiah's prophecies. Clearly, Jesus' fulfillment of prophecy was not going to match anyone's expectations—not even John's.

---

1. Matthew 11

2. 1 Kings 19

3. Isaiah 61:1 The Spirit of the Lord God is upon me, because the Lord has anointed me to bring good news to the poor; he has sent me to bind up the brokenhearted, to proclaim liberty to the captives, and the opening of the prison to those who are bound...

4. Isaiah 61:1; Isaiah 35:5-6 Then the eyes of the blind shall be opened, and the ears of the deaf unstopped; then shall the lame man leap like a deer, and the tongue of the mute sing for joy.

Then Jesus added a remarkable thing: "And blessed is the one who is not offended by me." No matter what blessings and miracles there are, you must still have faith. Even John the Baptist needed to have faith. Faith was required to accept that the Messiah was not as John or others imagined him from their reading and understanding of the Old Testament.

John the Baptist needed to be reminded that he did not have a shovel.[5] Our thinking about Jesus and his Kingdom must derive from what he actually said and did, and not from what we imagine he should be and do. Otherwise we will become demoralized as John was in prison.

Jesus then spoke to the crowd about John. He told them John's question did not flow from doubt about who Jesus was. John was not unstable or fickle, like a reed blown around in the wind. John's problem was that he was the last of the Old Covenant prophets. As such, he did not see the Kingdom with perfect clarity, even as the other Old Testament prophets failed to see the Kingdom clearly.

In the end, Jesus defended John. He reminded the people of their feelings when they went to see John in the wilderness; they were excited that God had again sent them a prophet. Yet John was more than a prophet because he was also the subject of prophecy. Not only did he come to proclaim God's word to Israel, the Old Testament prophets said he was a special prophet announcing the Day of the Lord. The Old Testament calls John the coming Elijah.[6]

The least is greater

John was the greatest Old Covenant prophet because he, more than any other prophet, most clearly identified Jesus as Messiah. However, Jesus said the one who is least in the Kingdom of God is greater than John.[7] Even the least person in the Kingdom can more clearly identify Jesus as King than John; and the least in the Kingdom is greater than any Old Covenant prophet because he has a better understanding of Jesus' Kingdom than any of them.

---

5. See Chapter 8: Not an Earthly Kingdom

6. Malachi 4:5-6; Matthew 11:14

7. Matthew 11:11 Truly, I say to you, among those born of women there has arisen no one greater than John the Baptist. Yet the one who is least in the kingdom of heaven is greater than he.

If you are in Jesus' Kingdom, you know Jesus as King better than John. You are not still wondering if Jesus is the Christ, or if you should be expecting someone else. No Christian (no one in the Kingdom) thinks that now. We know who the King is.

This teaches us a very significant truth about the Kingdom: If you are in the Kingdom, you must be pointing out who the King is. To be part of the Kingdom, you must proclaim the Kingdom. Telling others about the King and his Kingdom is an element of what it means to be in the Kingdom. Greatness in the Kingdom comes from telling others about the King and his Kingdom. If you do not reveal to others who the King is, what makes you think you are in the Kingdom?

John was the greatest prophet because he most clearly identified Jesus as King. Even in that, he still had difficulty fully understanding the King and the Kingdom. The least in the Kingdom of Heaven can more clearly tell others that Jesus is the King and that he has a Kingdom. The least in the Kingdom of God understands more about the Kingdom than John the Baptist did.

The role of John the Baptist

In the story of Jesus' transfiguration,[8] the disciples had an opportunity to see Jesus as he really was. While on a mountain with Peter, James, and John, Jesus was transfigured before them; his face shone like the sun and his clothes became white as light. Moses and Elijah also appeared, and God spoke from a bright cloud that overshadowed them, saying, "This is my beloved Son, with whom I am well pleased; listen to him."

Afterward, as they descended the mountain, the disciples asked Jesus about the coming of Elijah. There was clear belief that Elijah would come because of this specific prophecy:

> *Remember the law of my servant Moses, the statutes and rules that I commanded him at Horeb for all Israel. Behold, I will send you Elijah the prophet before the great and awesome day of the Lord comes. And he will turn the hearts of fathers to their children and the hearts of children to their fathers, lest I come and strike the land with a decree of utter destruction.*[9]

Basically, the disciples were asking, "If Elijah brings restoration,

8. Matthew 17
9. Malachi 4:4-6

then how come the Messiah dies?" It was a very good question. Jesus told his disciples that John the Baptist fulfilled the prophecy of Elijah. Even as John did his mission and died because of it, so also would the Messiah die doing his mission. To the disciples, this seemed like a strange idea of success.

The scribes also only understood this partially. Since they expected someone preparing for an earthly kingdom, they rejected John because he did not have a shovel. They erroneously assumed they would easily recognize Elijah, but instead they brought destruction on themselves by rejecting God's Kingdom.

John the Baptist's mission was to prepare the way for the Lord, showing the people who the King was. Once John was killed, this work would be taken up by Jesus' disciples.[10] To properly understand this, you must see the rest of the story as a living parable enacted before the disciples.

Restoring the child to the father

When Jesus, Peter, James and John returned from the mountain to the other disciples, they found a crowd gathered around a man who had come with his demonized son. Since nine disciples had been unable to drive the demon from the boy, Jesus rebuked them as faithless; then he proceeded to drive the demon out himself. He was upset with them because they were not able to restore the child to his father.

In Isaiah, within a context of God gathering the children of Israel back after judgment, we learn that there would be protection from water and fire.

> *When you pass through the waters, I will be with you; and through the rivers, they shall not overwhelm you; when you walk through fire you shall not be burned, and the flame shall not consume you.*[11]

This is precisely the method by which the demon was attempting to destroy the child—casting him into fire and water.[12] The text quoted above is found in the Isaiah section dealing with the coming of John the Baptist before Christ. That section begins with this:

---

10. cf. John 3:22-30; 4:2

11. Isaiah 43:2

12. Matthew 17:15 [The man] said, "Lord, have mercy on my son, for he is an epileptic and he suffers terribly. For often he falls into the fire, and often into the water."

> *A voice cries: "In the wilderness prepare the way of the Lord; make straight in the desert a highway for our God. Every valley shall be lifted up, and every mountain and hill be made low; the uneven ground shall become level, and the rough places a plain. And the glory of the Lord shall be revealed, and all flesh shall see it together, for the mouth of the Lord has spoken."*[13]

The work of Elijah is the work of John, restoring the children to the Father. This is what the living parable was all about. When Jesus came, he was able to restore the child to the father. The disciples were intended to take up the role of Elijah (John the Baptist) by faith. They were expected to restore the child to his father.

When the disciples asked why they were unable to cast the demon out, Jesus told them it was because they had little faith. The faith required to move mountains[14] is the same kind of faith with which John the Baptist came. As Jesus' disciples, we become the removers of mountains to prepare the way for the Lord.

The moving of mountains is not a physical moving of rock and dirt any more than Jesus' Kingdom is an earthly kingdom. Even as John did not come with a shovel, we do not need shovels. The mountains we move are the obstacles within the hearts of people that hinder them from coming to the King.

This whole story revolves around John the Baptist and his ministry. He came as Elijah, the one who would restore the hearts of the children to their fathers. He came to lead people to the King by removing mountains. Everyone in the Kingdom is now to work at introducing people to the King, and God promises that this work will happen *only* if we have faith.

Faith removes the mountains that hinder people from coming to the King. As Jesus' disciples, we take up the role of restoring people to God the Father. We do this by pointing out to people who the King is and by proclaiming the Gospel of the Kingdom. Fortunately, even the least in the Kingdom can point people to Christ better than John the Baptist.

---

13. Isaiah 40:3-5

14. Matthew 17:20 He said to them, "Because of your little faith. For truly, I say to you, if you have faith like a grain of mustard seed, you will say to this mountain, 'Move from here to there,' and it will move, and nothing will be impossible for you."

14 The Value System of the Kingdom

One of the most powerful discussions in which Jesus required the adoption of his value system for those in his Kingdom occurred when he was approached by a rich, young man.[1] The man asked Jesus what good deed he must do to have eternal life. Jesus responded by first pointing out that only God is good. He then pointed the young man to the commandments. If God is good and the commandments have come from God, then doing what the commandments require is what God expects of us. Being good is being like God. To have eternal life you must be like him in doing what is good.

Of course, the man wanted to know exactly which commandments he needed to keep. Jesus listed several of the Ten Commandments, finishing the list with "love your neighbor as yourself." Being good is not only about what you do *not* do. It is more about the *good that you do* to and for others.

The young man did not understand the point Jesus was making, so he claimed to have kept all the commandments Jesus listed. Although he was attempting to keep the Law, he remained empty inside because he failed to be like God. Keeping the Law only allows us to reflect the glory of God; it cannot change us to be like Christ.[2]

Therefore, Jesus gave the man homework that could bring about the desired change. He told the man to go and practice sacrificial love

1. Matthew 19:16-20:28
2. See Chapter 6: The Law Cannot Transform

for the benefit of others: "If you would be perfect, go, sell what you possess and give to the poor, and you will have treasure in heaven; and come, follow me."[3] In other words, do not merely *say* you love your neighbor, support your words with loving actions that *prove* you love your neighbor. Jesus did not want the man to merely follow rules that modified his behavior; he wanted the man's heart to change.

However, the man could not do what Jesus commanded because he loved his wealth and self more than he loved other people. Jesus taught that sacrificial love for others is the only way to come and follow him. To follow Jesus is to be like him, and to be like him is to be good like God. Until the man was willing to adopt Jesus' value system, he could not enter Jesus' Kingdom. The rich, young man chose emptiness and self rather than sacrifice and joy. Full of sorrow, he went away from Jesus that day; and Jesus let him go.

The young man was concerned about heaven and hell and eternal life, but the issue that Jesus focused on was whether the young man would be good; whether he would be like God. Jesus said that it is difficult for rich people to enter the Kingdom.[4] In fact, it is easier to stuff a camel through the eye of a needle than to get a rich person to adopt Jesus' value system. That statement should get our attention! It is extremely difficult to give up a value system that pampers one's self and move to a value system of self-sacrifice.

The Jews believed that having wealth was a sign of God's blessing; but Jesus taught that the more a person possessed, the harder it was to be a sacrificial lover, and the harder it was to be like God. Shocked by their misunderstanding of this idea, the disciples asked Jesus how anyone could be saved. Jesus replied that only with God's help could it be done. Remember, we need faith to walk where Jesus did. Sacrificial love for the benefit of others is as difficult as walking on water. We need God's help to exchange our value systems with his.

Peter then reminded Jesus that they had given up everything to follow him, and he wanted to know what they would receive in return. Peter was not claiming to have become a sacrificial lover with nothing left to give. Rather, he was saying, "This kingdom doesn't have any

---

3. Matthew 19:21

4. Matthew 19:23-24 And Jesus said to his disciples, "Truly, I say to you, only with difficulty will a rich person enter the kingdom of heaven. Again I tell you, it is easier for a camel to go through the eye of a needle than for a rich person to enter the kingdom of God."

money in it, does it Jesus?" Jesus essentially answered, "Nope, sorry. But, if you practice my value system, your relationships will be amazing and abundant." It was not an earthly kingdom, and it was not going to work out as Peter expected. He was expecting Jesus to have an earthly kingdom and, along with it, power and wealth.

A rich man like no other

In order to drive home his point, Jesus told them a little story. "The Kingdom of Heaven is like a rich man..." Wow! Jesus was not letting this go. To understand the parable correctly, we must relate it to both Peter's question and to the rich, young man who had recently departed. This is the only way to grasp Jesus' point. The story Jesus told was intended to demonstrate how much the rich, young man was unlike God by introducing another rich man—one unlike the disciples had ever experienced.[5]

The rich man in Jesus' story hired workers to harvest his vineyard at six in the morning. They agreed to work for a day and receive a day's wage. Through the course of that day, the man continued to hire more people every few hours. The unexpected twist in this story came when the rich man proceeded to pay his workers.

At the end of the day, he began paying the men he hired last; those who had only worked briefly. He gave them a whole day's wage for only a few hours work. He continued to pay each man a full day's wage even though he had hired them at different intervals throughout the day. When it came time for the first workers to be paid, their reward was the same as everyone else's. The rich man paid all the workers the same amount, regardless of how long they had served.

The men who had worked the whole day were upset because, having seen the generous pay offered all the other workers, they expected to receive more. They did not think they were treated fairly because they had worked harder and longer than everyone else. They became envious and jealous of those hired last, believing they deserved something more from the landowner. So the rich man asked the workers whether or not he was treating them unjustly. Was he cheating them by only paying them a day's wage?

What would you have done? You would have paid the men according to the percentage of the day they had worked, wouldn't you?

---

5. Matthew 20:1-16

But not this man. He was going to disrupt the whole economic situation! The man paid all his workers the same amount, regardless of the length of time they worked. They all received a full day's wage.

The rich man chose to pay those hired last the same amount as those hired first. It was his choice, for it was his money and he could choose to do with it as he pleased. He could be generous to whom he chose to be generous. Should the other workers be angry about the man's generosity?

The story reveals how God acts toward those who are in his Kingdom. The rich, young man who went away feeling sad was nothing like the rich man in Jesus' story. The story reveals how different God is in his Kingdom compared to the wealthy people of this world. He is willing to sacrifice for everyone in his Kingdom equally. This is not based on what they do for him, but based on his own generosity and his own value system. This is how the rich, young man needed to live in order to be like God. He needed to become generous in his concern for others if he wanted to be good.

In the days of this story, if a man did not work each day and receive payment, he and his family might not eat that day. If the rich man in the story had not paid the last workers a full day's wage, they or their families might not have had enough to eat that night. However, the story is not about how much money people should be paid.

This is a story about seeing someone else's need and meeting it. Those who worked the whole day had sufficient income to meet their need for the day. Those who worked only part of the day had the same amount of need, even though they had not done the same amount of labor. God, in his Kingdom, treats us based on our need, and not based on what we deserve. We all need eternal life, and God grants that to us graciously based on our need, and not according to what we do for him.

Jesus finished the story with "the last shall be first and the first last,"[6] which is the same thing he said to his disciples before he started the story.[7] This confirms the story was not only about the rich, young man to whom Jesus had first spoken, but also about the disciples. The story was intended for Peter who had asked, "There's no money in this, is there?" The story was about the sinful attitude of Jesus' disciples.

6. Matthew 20:16

7. Matthew 19:30

They believed they deserved more in the Kingdom because they had been with Jesus longer and had done more work for him. They had forgotten that everything in the Kingdom is about sacrificial love, of God's mercy and grace, and *not* about what we deserve. The disciples who followed Jesus first were not to expect anything more than anyone else in the Kingdom—yet they did expect more. This was essentially what Peter meant: "I deserve more than the next guy." The attitude of "I do more for God" is not an attitude of the Kingdom. It is not part of the value system of the Kingdom.

When we believe we should get more from God than others, we have forgotten that all we have received is through sacrificial love on his part. It is not based on what we deserve or on the work we have done. We have abundantly experienced the generosity of our God, and it far outweighs any effort on our part.

To be like God, we need to treat others based on their need and not by what they deserve. The greater the need, the greater the sacrifice required. Those who came to the field late still needed to be paid in order to eat that night. If they received less than a full day's wage, either they or their families would go hungry. The master was not about to let that happen. He gave them all a day's wage because that was what they all needed. The landowner would be rewarded in terms of relationship by thankful people.

The disciples discovered they were a lot more like the rich, young man than they were like Jesus, because they shared the same heart attitude as the rich, young man. The only difference between them was that he had money and they did not. They both shared an attitude that was the opposite of Jesus'. None of them were motivated by sacrificial love for the benefit of others.

Instead of understanding the message, the disciples continued to bicker over who would gain the privileged positions in the Kingdom.[8] Jesus told his disciples he would be rejected, mocked, flogged and crucified. In spite of this picture of being raised up on a cross, the mother of James and John came to plead for them to have the right and left hand positions next to Jesus. She was thinking of honored positions in the Kingdom, but imagining Jesus hanging on a cross with men on either side helps you realize how much the disciples did not grasp what Jesus was saying to them.

8. Matthew 20:20-28

Jesus was unable to offer the men positions of honor according to their own terms. Instead, he offered greatness according to his own standard. They could serve others, even to the point of suffering and death, and thereby be great according to Christ. Jesus is greatest in his Kingdom because he is the greatest servant. To be great in God's eyes is to become like Christ, giving up your life sacrificially for others.

15 The King Revealed

Jesus made his final, spectacular entry into Jerusalem in the full style of a King.[1] He had his disciples fetch a donkey, the symbol of David's kingship, which he rode into the city. The crowds put branches on the road and called out, "Hosanna to the Son of David! Blessed is he who comes in the name of the Lord! Hosanna in the highest!"

Immediately after his triumphal entrance, Jesus entered the temple and drove out those who were selling in the temple courts. He did this because the true purpose of the temple was to provide a place of worship, but it had become a chaotic marketplace, possibly with corrupt trade practices that exploited others. Since this was immediately prior to the Passover, it was a direct affront to the temple authorities. They were outraged at Jesus!

In explaining his actions, Jesus quoted[2] the prophets to reveal how the temple was intended for all peoples[3] and how the true purpose of the temple had been subverted.[4] Instead of being the place where people could come in pure worship of God, it had become a tool for

1. Matthew 21

2. Matthew 21:13 He said to them, "It is written, 'My house shall be called a house of prayer,' but you make it a den of robbers."

3. Isaiah 56:7 ...these I will bring to my holy mountain, and make them joyful in my house of prayer; their burnt offerings and their sacrifices will be accepted on my altar; for my house shall be called a house of prayer for all peoples.

4. Jeremiah 7:11 Has this house, which is called by my name, become a den of robbers in your eyes? Behold, I myself have seen it, declares the Lord.

arousing people to nationalism. Rather than bringing universal salvation, it brought political exclusivism.

Jesus' criticism becomes especially evident once we realize this trade was occurring where the Gentiles were expected to worship God! The Jews did not care if someone's worship of God was hindered, as long as that someone was a Gentile. After all, they reasoned, this was the Jewish God and the Jewish temple.

Though now at the temple, the children were still calling out, "Hosanna to the Son of David!" continuing the chants that began with his entry into Jerusalem. Jesus accepted their statement of him being the Messiah, furthering the indignance of the authorities. By quoting, "Out of the mouth of infants and nursing babies you have prepared praise,"[5] Jesus silenced his critics, which allowed the people to continue praising him without fear. Although the Psalm was about praising God, the hosannas of the children were given to the Son of David. Jesus is the King of the Kingdom of God, and he accepts the praise due God alone. He does this because he is God.

Moving mountains

After they left the temple, Jesus enacted a parable of judgment for the disciples to witness. He approached a fig tree in full leaf, which normally indicated fruitfulness. Finding no fruit on the tree, Jesus cursed it, causing it to wither. The fig tree was like the sellers in the temple and those trying to silence the praise of the children. They pretended to be pious, but it was an external, fruitless act.

When the disciples asked how the tree withered so quickly, Jesus answered, "Truly, I say to you, if you have faith and do not doubt, you will not only do what has been done to the fig tree, but even if you say to this mountain, 'Be taken up and thrown into the sea,' it will happen. And whatever you ask in prayer, you will receive, if you have faith."[6]

The withering of the tree indicates judgment for lack of fruitfulness, and the removal of mountains by faith is, as we have previously seen, the preparation for the coming of the Messiah. The meaning of this becomes easily understood once we see what immediately followed.

5. Psalm 8:2

6. Matthew 21:21-22

The chief priests asked Jesus whose authority permitted him to bring judgment to the temple.[7] He answered only by reference to the ministry of John the Baptist. Remember, John's ministry was to move mountains and prepare for the coming of the King. If the leaders would acknowledge that John came from God, the mountains in their hearts would move. If they did not, they would be cursed like the fig tree.

Those two options were all they had. They could, by faith, have the mountains moved and receive the Messiah. Or they could continue the charade of leafy, fruitless trees and be cursed by God. The chief priests and elders would not answer Jesus' question about whether or not John the Baptist came from God, because they were either not ready for, or not wanting, God's Messiah.

After that, Jesus told them a parable about a man who had two sons whom he had asked to work in his vineyard. Each son responded differently to his father's request. One stated he would not work, but later changed his mind and did his father's will. The second son promised to obey, but in the end, rebelled against his father.

Of course, the parable referred to the ministry of John the Baptist. The tax collectors and sinners believed John, accepted the removal of mountains, and entered the Kingdom by faith. They were like the son who began defiant, but later honored his father's wishes. However, the religious leaders who pretended to do God's will remained cursed and did not have the mountains in their hearts removed. The path between them and the King remained blocked.

Jesus then told another parable, making this even more specific.[8] In it he revealed the method and outcome of those who wished to kill him. Jesus told of a landowner who leased a vineyard to some tenants. When the time for harvest arrived, the tenants refused to give the landowner his share of the crop. Instead, they beat and killed not only the servants who were sent, but also the landowner's son.

Even as Jesus spoke this parable to them, murder was in their hearts because they refused to accept him as the Son. They did not want this Messiah! They preferred to rule themselves. Not only was this the actual case of the temple leaders who did not believe the prophecies about a Messiah, it is the heart of everyone who chooses his own value system over the King's.

---

7. Matthew 21:23-27
8. Matthew 21:33-46

Jesus then quoted a Psalm[9] that spoke prophetically of his death as the Son. Not only would he die as the Son, but as the Psalm proclaimed, he would also live. The tenants in the story were the religious leaders who would be crushed and have the Kingdom given to others.

Continuing his teaching against the chief priests, Jesus told of a king who gave a wedding feast for his son.[10] In this story, those invited to the celebration refused to come, choosing either to ignore the invitation or to mistreat the king's messengers. Refusing a wedding invitation is a rejection of those involved in the wedding. Jesus was telling his hearers that refusing him was refusing the King; something that would result in judgment.

The beautiful part of this story is how the king now permitted everyone to come to his son's wedding feast. The servants were told to go out and invite anyone they could find. The doors were open to everyone, and both the good *and the bad* were allowed to attend the feast. The king welcomed everyone, even those who previously did not keep the law. Of course, this parable is about the rejection of Christ by the Jews and the subsequent invitation to all people.

At this point, the story takes an ominous turn—someone was found without a wedding garment. Attending a wedding requires that you adopt garments fitting the occasion. In the same way—and this is Jesus' final point—only those who are willing to adopt the values of the Kingdom can remain in the Kingdom. You cannot show up only for the food while rejecting the spirit of the occasion in your heart. Jesus made a very significant point about his Kingdom with this story. One does not enter the Kingdom by keeping the law, but by accepting the King and the value system of his Kingdom.

9. Psalm 118:22-23 The stone that the builders rejected has become the cornerstone. This is the Lord's doing; it is marvelous in our eyes.

10. Matthew 22:1-14

16 The Spiritual Kingdom

Seeking to trap or discredit Jesus, his various opponents came to him asking questions in line with their specific ideas of the Messiah.[1] In each case it betrayed their misunderstanding of the nature of the Kingdom of God. Although Jesus consistently preached that he was the King of the Kingdom of God, they failed to accept him in that role based on their misunderstanding of the Scriptures.

The first to speak were the Pharisees and Herodians,[2] who teamed up to ask a question revolving around the legality of taxes. Should a Jew pay taxes to the Roman Caesar? This was obviously a trap. If Jesus supported the tax it would undermine his position before the people, for paying the tax was unpopular and would indicate he supported Roman rule. However, if he rejected it, the Herodians were standing ready to accuse him of treason and report him to the Romans.

Calling for a Roman coin, Jesus pointed out that since the coin and its inscription were clearly Caesar's, it ultimately belonged to Caesar and not to them. The Jew who paid taxes to such a man was openly declaring he was under God's judgment; for any Jew who paid it was not in a free kingdom, but was under the authority of another nation. Paying taxes to Caesar was an acknowledgment that the people of Israel were still in exile, even if living in their own land.

---

1. Matthew 22:15-46

2. Herodians were interested in political stability, not religion. They supported Roman taxation.

Jesus said that since the coin had Caesar's name on it, it must be his: "Therefore render to Caesar the things that are Caesar's, and to God the things that are God's." By answering as he did, Jesus declared he would not be a political messiah or revolutionary. He was interested only in building the Kingdom of God. He called people to acknowledge that they were made in God's image, and they should bear that image fully, through adopting God's value system.

The Sadducees, who rejected both the idea of a Messiah in the line of David and belief in a resurrection from the dead, asked Jesus a theological question in an attempt to mock the idea of resurrection. Ignoring their mockery, Jesus told them that once a person experiences resurrection, everything changes. God's power brings something greater than what was previously seen or experienced. Humorously, Jesus compared those resurrected by God to angels, yet another thing the Sadducees did not believe in!

Jesus finished by quoting part of the Old Testament they did accept.[3] The promises of God to Abraham, Isaac, and Jacob are written in a way that declared the men were not dead but still alive.[4] If God promises to be someone's God, the promise does not cease with the physical death of the believer and recipient of promise. God will resurrect a person to keep his promise and continue being his God. Belief in resurrection is an absolutely essential requirement for participation in Christ's Kingdom.

The Pharisees then sent a teacher of the law to ask Jesus which was the greatest commandment in the Law. They either asked this question because they did not know the answer or because they were sure his answer would be wrong. Jesus answered that loving the Lord God with all your heart, with all your soul, and with all your mind was the greatest and first commandment. God must be first and foremost. However, Jesus did not leave it at that. He tied our love for God to our love for our neighbors: "And the second is like it: You shall love your neighbor as yourself." How else can we show our love for God in this world if not by being like him in loving others as he has loved us?

Note that the love Jesus taught is active love and not passive. He

3. The Sadducees regarded only the Law (Genesis-Deuteronomy) as authoritative, rejecting the historical and prophetical portions of the Old Testament. This outlook prevented them from believing in the Davidic Covenant and the Messiah.

4. Matthew 22:32 I am the God of Abraham, and the God of Isaac, and the God of Jacob.

set a positive command (what we must do) rather than a negative one (what we must not do). Jesus did not give his disciples a list of rules to follow, but claimed loving one another would automatically complete all the rules and fulfill God's value system. This is the same as saying that the Gospel has two parts to it: a part that we believe and a part that we do. We demonstrate our belief in God by loving our neighbor. Without love for God and man, the Bible becomes worthless to us and the message dead. This is what was wrong with the Pharisees and Sadducees.

Finally, Jesus asked them a question: "Whose son is the Christ?" When they answered that the Messiah was the son of David, Jesus asked how David could call his own son "Lord."[5] Under what circumstance could the king call his own son Lord? They should have concluded that the Christ was not only the son of David, but also the son of David's Lord—the Son of God. But they would never say it. In Jesus, the human son and the divine Son are brought together. He is the human son of David, but he is also the divine Son of God.

The questions in this section reveal why these men failed to recognize Jesus as the Messiah. They were focused on earthly things, whereas Jesus' Kingdom is spiritual. They thought of taxes, while his Kingdom is not an earthly kingdom and does not have taxes or an earthly ruler. They rejected resurrection, yet his Kingdom would be built on God's promise to raise the dead. Resurrection changes everything about how you live: Will you build yourself an earthly kingdom or place your trust in a Kingdom you cannot see, and that you only fully inherit when you die? The question about which law was the greatest had an earthly focus, whereas in Jesus' Kingdom, love is the single rule. Laws are for earthly kingdoms, but love is for Christ's spiritual Kingdom. You cannot make people love one another by law. Ultimately, the men were expecting a human messiah and were not ready to accept a divine one; Jesus did not match their ideas of God.

After that, Jesus warned his disciples concerning the scribes and Pharisees,[6] and pronounced seven woes against them for the following actions.[7] First, they kept Jews out of the Kingdom by rejecting and teaching others to reject the King. Second, they kept Gentiles from

5. Psalm 110:1 The Lord says to my Lord: "Sit at my right hand, until I make your enemies your footstool."

6. Matthew 23:1-12

7. Matthew 23:13-36

the Messiah. Third, they kept the people's focus on rules rather than on God. Fourth, they kept the details of the Law while not adopting God's values of justice, mercy, and faithfulness. They tried to keep the Law without being like the Lawmaker. That is why they were able to miss the Messiah standing before them—they did not share a common value system with him. Fifth, they kept rules, but missed the moral point of them all. Sixth, they looked good on the outside, but were spiritually gruesome inside. And seventh, morally they were the descendants of those who killed the prophets, and they would ultimately prove this by killing God's Messiah.

The woes against the scribes and Pharisees all boil down to their rejection of the King, his Kingdom, and the value system of his Kingdom. The only means by which we may escape the wrath of God is by accepting the King, adopting his value system, and entering his Kingdom.

Life in the Kingdom

Matthew chapters 24 and 25 must be read together as one unit. Without going into detail on all aspects of this section, I want to point out what relates specifically to Christ's Kingdom. First, many misunderstand the disciples' question, resulting in a misinterpretation of the entire passage. When the disciples asked, "Tell us, when will these things be, and what will be the sign of your coming and of the close of the age?" they were not asking about a second coming, but a coming to power in an earthly kingdom.

In other words, they were asking about Christ's *first* coming, without any clue about a second coming at all. His disciples were *still* thinking in terms of an earthly kingdom. We must keep this in mind when reading these chapters. It helps us understand that throughout chapter 24, Jesus was outlining events that would transpire in the realm of earthly kingdoms, but these were not to be mistaken with what was occurring within his spiritual Kingdom.

During the course of the events Jesus warned about,[8] the disciples were to live according to his instructions on how to treat one another while waiting for the return of their King.[9] First, anyone who abused members of the Kingdom would find, in the end, they were not part

8. Matthew 24:4-44

9. Matthew 24:45-25:46

of it.[10] There is a behavioral requirement for all those in the Kingdom, and it is to care for all others in the Kingdom.

How we treat the members of the Kingdom reveals whether or not we are truly in it. If you are in God's Kingdom, you will treat all other members of the Kingdom with sacrificial love. You cannot separate your personal beliefs from the actions that flow from them. You will live your value system. And if the value system you live is not the one of the Kingdom, you are not part of it.

Second, in the parable of the ten virgins,[11] Jesus taught his disciples to be prepared while waiting for their King. Those who are prepared cannot help those who are unprepared. Waiting for the King is an individual responsibility. The foolish virgins thought that waiting would be easy and failed to enter the Kingdom.

Third, we learn that God expects us to work while we wait for the King.[12] Doing nothing in the Kingdom implies you do not trust the Master. Waiting for the coming of the King requires that we be active, advancing his Kingdom while we wait for his return. The wicked servant did nothing because he thought serving the Master was too difficult; he was paralyzed by fear and unbelief.

Many Christians mistakenly believe that Jesus' Kingdom is some future event for them. Instead, they need to realize they are in Christ's Kingdom *right now.* We are expected to expand his Kingdom by helping others enter it, and by sacrificially loving those within it who are in need.

---

10. Matthew 24:45-51

11. Matthew 25:1-13

12. Matthew 25:14-30

17 The Rejection of the King

Jesus told his disciples that his death would coincide with the Passover, not only in time, but in theme. As the Israelites were celebrating God's deliverance of them from Egypt, Jesus died to release us from bondage to sin. This was a crucial part of the Kingdom plan.

The priests were active, gathering to plot the murder of Jesus.[1] Initially, they desired to kill Jesus after, not during, the feast. But God overruled their plans. The death of Christ was not scheduled by the will of man, but by the will of God.

The Kingdom issue in this section flows from the motive of the priests. They desired the death of Jesus because they rejected him as the Messiah and King. They considered him a troublemaker who would bring instability and damage their position (their kingdom) under their Roman masters.

Preparation for Jesus' death came through an unexpected, generous anointing. A woman wishing to express the depths of her love for him poured a flask of very expensive perfume on his head. Jesus willingly accepted this honor, but the financial waste disturbed Judas. God's plan was set in motion through the woman's sacrificial love for Jesus. Judas' negative reaction to the woman's value system prompted him to fulfill God's design.

We do not fully know why Judas chose to betray Jesus. Certainly, the underlying reason was his disappointment with *this* Messiah, *this*

1. Matthew 26

King. Jesus was not turning out to be the kind of king Judas wished to follow. When one becomes disappointed with the true King, he will always seek a poor substitute. Since Judas was willing to betray Jesus for so small a price, it is also possible he may have been trying to force Jesus' hand, pressing him to begin a fight for an earthly kingdom.

Though previously fearing a riot during the feast, the priests decided that with Judas' help they could safely arrest and kill Jesus. Finding and identifying someone in the first century was not as easy as in the present day. There were no pictures of Jesus, so the easiest way to arrest him privately was to use an inside man to reveal their target at a specific time and location. Guided by Judas, they could arrest Jesus away from any crowds who might support him.

During Jesus' last meal with his disciples, he revealed knowledge of his betrayer. Jesus was moving events toward the full establishment of his Kingdom. Over and over again, we are given information that proves God was fulfilling his plan, and that Jesus was not a victim of circumstances beyond his control.

God's plan also involved the scattering of Jesus' disciples. This would ultimately protect them from danger, but their scattering also demonstrated their own rejection of Jesus as Messiah. Even though Jesus told them what would happen that night, his disciples were not prepared for how suddenly it would all transpire. Peter claimed he was willing to suffer for Jesus and fight for him and his Kingdom. Jesus, however, predicted Peter's threefold denial of him that very night. Peter was still unaware of how Jesus' Kingdom worked and extended. It grows not through the sword, but through sacrificial love.

Jesus' prayer in Gethsemane revealed the great sorrow he had as he anticipated the cross.[2] His death would be like no other. Not only would he suffer and die under the wrath of God, his perfect relationship with the Father would be broken. He struggled because the greatest relationship had to briefly be severed in order to restore our broken relationships with God. Thus, he faced his greatest temptation: would he do the Father's will or not?

This, again, is really a question of Kingdom. Even as he faced the

2. Matthew 26:38-39 Then he said to them, "My soul is very sorrowful, even to death; remain here, and watch with me." And going a little farther he fell on his face and prayed, saying, "My Father, if it be possible, let this cup pass from me; nevertheless, not as I will, but as you will."

devil in the wilderness, or when Peter challenged Jesus' prediction to die in this way,[3] Jesus faced the possibility of a kingdom by means other than sacrificial love. He could certainly have an earthly kingdom and avoid the cross, but it would not be a kingdom worth possessing.

Jesus reminded his disciples to pray concerning the temptation to fall away that night. Through Jesus' own prayer, and the prayer to which he called his disciples, we learn the chief purpose for prayer. Prayer prepares us for sacrificial love—the will of the Father. Jesus was ready for the sacrifice of the cross *through prayer*, whereas his disciples were not ready because they had not prayed to be prepared. We do not receive whatever we desire through prayer, even as Jesus could not avoid the cross through prayer. But we can receive the power and strength of God to face taking up our crosses because the prayer of transformation to Christ-likeness is something God always promises to answer.[4]

When Judas led the Jews to Jesus in order to arrest him, Peter tried to prove his faithfulness with a sword. Jesus stopped him because his Kingdom is not an earthly kingdom and cannot be established or extended in the ways of earthly kingdoms. If any life is to be laid down it is not our enemies', but our own.

Once the Jews arrested Jesus, he was taken before the high priest. Although they accused him of many crimes in order to establish guilt, they had already decided against him. Jesus was silent before them until the high priest asked if he was the Christ, the Son of God.[5] Jesus answered affirmatively while announcing his ascension to the throne of the Kingdom of God.[6]

Prior to this, they desired his death; but with those words they wanted to kill him immediately. The Jewish leaders feared losing the power they had under Roman rule. They had to reject Jesus as king because they believed any attempt on his part to establish an earthly kingdom would create conflict with the Romans. Their fears were based on a misunderstanding of the nature of the Kingdom. Though

---

3. Matthew 16:21-23 (see Chapter 12: The Keys to the Kingdom)

4. See Chapter 29: Prayer and Sacrificial Love

5. Matthew 26:63 But Jesus remained silent. And the high priest said to him, "I adjure you by the living God, tell us if you are the Christ, the Son of God."

6. Matthew 26:64 Jesus said to him, "You have said so. But I tell you, from now on you will see the Son of Man seated at the right hand of Power and coming on the clouds of heaven."

they wanted to kill Jesus, the Jews did not have authority to do it in the manner they desired. Crucifying Jesus required the help of their Roman oppressors, so they took Jesus to Pilate, the Roman governor.

Pilate asked Jesus if he was the king of the Jews, and Jesus answered that he was. However, when the Jews variously accused Jesus, he again became silent. This behavior amazed Pilate, since anyone accused of being king of the Jews faced serious consequences before the Romans, and those accused of wrongdoing usually defended themselves.

Did the Roman governor think Jesus was king of the Jews? No. If Jesus wanted to make trouble and fight against the Romans, he was far too quiet and polite to Pilate, the Roman authority. Pilate had experience with radical Jews ranting before him. Jesus was not like them at all.

Each year at the Passover feast, the Roman governor released a prisoner as a sign of good will toward the Jews. Those present were supporters of Barabbas, another prisoner detained on charges of insurrection (an attempt to establish an earthly kingdom). The Jewish leaders caused them to call for Barabbas to be released and for Jesus to be crucified. Asking for Barabbas to be released and Jesus to be crucified revealed how much more the Jewish leaders feared Jesus than Barabbas. Regardless of how much the crowd knew of Jesus, their calls for Barabbas' freedom spoke of whom they preferred and the kind of kingdom for which they hoped. They would rather have Barabbas' earthly kingdom than the spiritual one Jesus offered.

The Roman soldiers responsible for executing Jesus mocked him and beat him. They put a crown of thorns on his head, spit on him, and cried out, "Hail king of the Jews!" It was their way of showing how much they hated Jews and how they scoffed at the idea of Jews having their own kingdom.

The Jewish priests and the Romans both wanted Jesus crucified in order to prove exactly the same point: Jesus was definitely *not* the king of the Jews. Instead, crucifixion would demonstrate to all that Jesus was cursed by God.[7]

---

7. Deuteronomy 21:22-23 And if a man has committed a crime punishable by death and he is put to death, and you hang him on a tree, his body shall not remain all night on the tree, but you shall bury him the same day, for a hanged man is cursed by God. You shall not defile your land that the Lord your God is giving you for an inheritance.

But do not forget that it was also God's plan for Jesus to be crucified. God intended for Jesus to die on a cross to show that Jesus *was* cursed by God in order to remove the curse against us.[8] God wanted to show his absolute love for us and demonstrate his value system. God wanted to show his power over sin and death. And finally, Jesus wanted to show that his Kingdom was not of this world.[9]

When the Jews rejected Jesus, they rejected him as their king and could not enter his Kingdom. Jesus is a King and he has a Kingdom. We demonstrate we are in it by adopting his value system and obeying him as King. We can enter God's Kingdom and live by his value system, or we can remain in our own kingdoms and live by our own choices. Every time we pick our own kingdom, we pick rebellion against God and his Kingdom. Every time we choose to avoid suffering and avoid being like Jesus, we choose our kingdom. Every time we do this, we yell, "Release Barabbas, we want him as king. Crucify Jesus!" Every time we disobey him, we mock his kingship and admit which kind of kingdom we really desire.

We must keep these questions in mind all of the time: Is Jesus my King? Do I show love as he did? Do I help others as he did? Or, do I put myself first and want the best for me? Do I want to have an earthly kingdom, or be in his spiritual Kingdom?

8. Galatians 3:13 Christ redeemed us from the curse of the law by becoming a curse for us—for it is written, "Cursed is everyone who is hanged on a tree"...

9. John 18:36 Jesus answered, "My kingdom is not of this world. If my kingdom were of this world, my servants would have been fighting, that I might not be delivered over to the Jews. But my kingdom is not from the world."

18 The Establishment of the Kingdom

Jesus established his Kingdom through his death and resurrection. Anything that rejects Christ's death and resurrection is not Christian, for the death and resurrection of Christ are inseparable from Christianity. The cross and the empty tomb have always been powerful symbols in the lives of Christians because all our hope rests on what happened there.

Death

When Jesus died on the cross,[1] the written charge against him was posted above his head: "King of the Jews." Yes, he was and is the King, but he was King in ways unimaginable to all those who killed him.

Jews mocked him and said, "If you are the Son of God, come down, save yourself." It was like his temptation by the devil at the beginning, "If you are the Son of God..." Jesus heard these words of the devil over and over, but he knew, even as he hung on the cross, *it is better to be good than to have your bodily needs met, and to have people like you, and to have power and an earthly kingdom.* Hanging on a cross was the ultimate expression of losing control over bodily appetites, being rejected by others, and being completely powerless.

Others said, "He saved others; he cannot save himself." They meant this to indicate his powerlessness, but Jesus knew that only through sacrificial love could he save others. One cannot sacrifice for others

1. Matthew 27:32-54

and live selfishly at the same time. They also said, "If he comes down off the cross, we will believe he is the king." Yet coming down would only establish an earthly kingdom, while staying on the cross established his spiritual Kingdom.

Finally, Jesus spoke: "My God, why have you forsaken me?" God the Father turned his back on his Son so he could turn his face toward us. To be blessed is to have God's face shine upon you, but to be cursed is to have him turn away from you and reject you.[2] Jesus experienced rejection that we might be accepted. The curse of God is rejection by God; it is relational death and spiritual death. The perfect relationship between Father and Son was severed so that God's face might be turned toward those who first turned their backs to him.

A Roman soldier, standing near the cross when Jesus died, was filled with awe and said, "Truly this was the Son of God." God's value system is sacrificial love for the benefit of others. It most looks like Jesus on the cross. God's love is most revealed by Jesus' death on the cross. And Jesus is most readily identified as the Son of God in his death on the cross.

Was it easy for Jesus to die on the cross? No. Sacrificial love for the benefit of others is difficult—as difficult as walking on water. We can only do it by faith in the promise of God's resurrection. We can only do it if we believe in a God who raises the dead.

Jesus' sacrifice was great. In fact, it was the greatest sacrifice ever made. Remember, the greater the need, the greater the sacrifice. Our need was so great it could only be met by the sacrifice of God's own Son. How can we ever think we can help ourselves with a need of that magnitude?

Resurrection

The chief priests and Pharisees came before Pilate to ask for security around Jesus' tomb,[3] but it was not belief in Jesus' claim to rise from the dead that motivated them. What really worried them was the fear that the disciples would steal Jesus' body and then claim he had been

2. Numbers 6:22-27 The Lord spoke to Moses, saying, "Speak to Aaron and his sons, saying, Thus you shall bless the people of Israel: you shall say to them, The Lord bless you and keep you; the Lord make his face to shine upon you and be gracious to you; the Lord lift up his countenance upon you and give you peace. So shall they put my name upon the people of Israel, and I will bless them."

3. Matthew 27:62-66

raised from the dead. Their fears were a bit misplaced, considering how shocked the disciples were concerning Jesus' sudden crucifixion. Even the disciples did not understand or wish to accept a dying Messiah until they themselves became convinced of his resurrection.

Jesus was buried and then rose from the dead on the third day. This is very important because it demonstrates that Jesus has power over death. *We must believe in a God who raises the dead.* We must have faith in his promise to raise us up from the grave, even as he was raised.

Sacrificial love for others draws its energy from faith in resurrection. If we think death is the end, we may be hesitant to sacrifice our lives; but Jesus shows us we have nothing to fear by living sacrificially since he has already proven his power over death.

Commission

The last scene in the book of Matthew depicts Jesus sending his disciples into the world.[4] He told them, "All authority in heaven and on earth has been given to me." This is the language of a Kingdom—the greatest Kingdom there will ever be. After his resurrection, Jesus' Kingdom had fully come.

Because the Kingdom was now established, he commanded his disciples to go and make more disciples. This is the task of everyone in the Kingdom. The two aspects of making a disciple are baptizing and teaching.

The idea of baptism should remind us of John the Baptist. John's purpose was to make straight the way for the Lord. He prepared people's hearts for the King. So, the Great Commission is the same as John the Baptist's mission. The disciples must continue to do the work John started. Everyone in Christ's Kingdom should be preparing the hearts of people for the King. They are not to be creating an earthly kingdom.

We are also called to teach people to observe all that Jesus commanded. And that, of course, is his value system: sacrificial love for the benefit of others. Not only are we to live it, we are to teach it to others.

4. Matthew 28:18-20 And Jesus came and said to them, "All authority in heaven and on earth has been given to me. Go therefore and make disciples of all nations, baptizing them in the name of the Father and of the Son and of the Holy Spirit, teaching them to observe all that I have commanded you. And behold, I am with you always, to the end of the age."

The King and his Kingdom

This brief overview of the Kingdom from the book of Matthew teaches us these lessons about the King and the Kingdom:

- Jesus is the King of the Kingdom of God.
- Jesus' Kingdom is a spiritual Kingdom, not an earthly kingdom.
- We must adopt the value system of the King to enter his Kingdom.
- Jesus' Kingdom is for all people, not only Jews.
- To enter Jesus' Kingdom, you must recognize that his authority comes from God.
- Only those who believe Jesus has authority to forgive sins can enter his Kingdom.
- Those in the Kingdom must be forgiving.
- To be part of the Kingdom, you must proclaim the Kingdom. Greatness in the Kingdom comes from telling others about the King and his Kingdom.
- Faith is required to follow Jesus because living sacrificial love all the time is as difficult as walking on water.
- You must believe in a God who raises the dead. Jesus was raised to life so that those in his Kingdom need not fear death.

Part 3: The Gospel of the Kingdom

19 Only One Gospel

The Gospel is comprised of two parts: a doctrine we must believe and the resultant action accompanying that belief. To say it with more simplicity: *a part that we believe and a part that we do*. It is not only something we believe, nor is it only something we do. Both what we believe and what we do form one complete belief in one complete Gospel.

Perhaps it is better to use the word "acknowledge" when speaking of the parts of our Faith that we hold to be true. Customarily we use the word "believe," yet that lessens the biblical idea of belief. Belief (or faith) as taught in the Bible is more than what you acknowledge to be true. It includes the actions that accompany those acknowledgements. Together, what we acknowledge and what we do is our faith. They are one inseparable whole. You cannot acknowledge something as true without acting according to that acknowledgement.

The danger of a false gospel

If nothing else, Paul believed in the Gospel. He believed there was one *and only one* true message of the cross. Of course, he also believed that a wrong message could be proclaimed, resulting in tragic consequences.[1]

1. Galatians 1:6-9 I am astonished that you are so quickly deserting him who called you in the grace of Christ and are turning to a different gospel—not that there is another one, but there are some who trouble you and want to distort the gospel of Christ. But even if we or an angel from heaven should preach to you a gospel contrary

If it is possible to proclaim a false gospel, then we must make certain that what we believe, teach, and proclaim is indeed the one true Gospel—nothing more and nothing less. There is a danger in too little as well as too much. We must not omit any crucial element, nor add additional requirements as indicators of orthodoxy.

Getting the Gospel right is crucial for salvation. When we add anything to it, we tend to create hindrances for fellowship with other believers, and we are in danger of substituting God's Gospel for a gospel of our own creation. In the end, we call sin what God does not, we destroy relationships, and we proclaim a false message about Christ's Kingdom.

Christians must be very careful not to confuse application of the Gospel for the Gospel. When we erroneously add application of the Gospel to it, we change the Gospel by intertwining it with ideas that are separate or foreign to it.

For example, an application of the Gospel is a specific way in which we ought to behave in a particular circumstance or culture at a given point in history and time. Though it may relate to our dress or speech, we can never add those manners to the Gospel by making them a measure of salvation or faith. They might be an application of how the Gospel compels us to treat one another, but they are not the Gospel. The Gospel requires that we love one another, but the loving action is determined by circumstances such as the needs around us and our ability to meet them.

The greatest problems of Christian unity flow from traditions and interpretations that may once have arisen from an application of the Gospel, but are now confused with the Gospel itself. Taking ideas from a New Testament application of the Gospel (how the Gospel applied to life in the early Church) and treating those ideas as though they are the Gospel (what must be done in order to be a believer) is wrong.

In seeking to know the Gospel, we must be careful not to include in our definition everything we find in the Bible. Head coverings, dress codes for women, and other traditions may be in the Bible, but are they the Gospel? If so, we must keep them like law for salvation, fearful we will be lost should we fail to keep all the rules. If they are

---

to the one we preached to you, let him be accursed. As we have said before, so now I say again: If anyone is preaching to you a gospel contrary to the one you received, let him be accursed.

not part of the Gospel, we must know why it was applied in that way for that particular time, place, and culture.

Lack of discernment in separating Gospel from application is one of the identifying marks of legalism and divisiveness within the Church. If we teach our traditions and interpretations as part of the Gospel, they become the new basis for fellowship and salvation. They become our gospel. It is crucially important to recognize this error since Paul made it quite clear that the Gospel could be distorted by adding to it, thus making it no Gospel at all. Distorting the Gospel by adding to it or changing it places you under a curse.

Being sure of the Gospel

In order to determine and separate the Gospel from the New Testament application of it, we must examine the core ideas present in the Gospel Jesus taught and the Gospel Paul taught. The similarities are the Gospel, while other ideas are application of the Gospel. Even though Jesus and Paul used different language and emphasis, the Gospel they taught was exactly the same.

For Jesus' teaching, I will summarize the ideas I have presented in previous chapters. For Paul, I will discuss which elements he taught were absolutely necessary components of the Gospel. They form a list from which nothing could be taken away without Paul declaring the teaching to be a false gospel. Unsurprisingly, our "must have" list from Paul will mesh perfectly with the essentials from Jesus' teaching.

Each theme established by Jesus and recorded by Matthew is in Paul's discussion of the Gospel. Jesus and Paul completely agree on the central concepts of the King and his Kingdom. What differs is the language and expression of Paul. He spoke less in Kingdom terminology and more in terms of relationship. As we explore his language, it will become quite clear that the basic principles of the Kingdom are relational.

Although Paul offered significant application of the Gospel, it is not difficult to determine what he considered crucial for salvation. He was very clear about what needed to be affirmed in his Gospel, and he laid down requirements for belief and action.

In his letter to the Galatians, who were in danger of turning to a false gospel, Paul argued that what happened to him on the road to

Damascus was the Gospel.[2] In his meeting with Jesus, every element Paul later championed as the Gospel was revealed to him. First, Christ was revealed to him as the King. Second, salvation was found in grace and not works of the Law. Third, resurrection was available to all those who followed the Christ who had power over sin and death. Fourth, the Gospel was for all people, Jew and Gentile. And fifth, Paul needed to replace his value system with God's value system. Amazingly, but not surprisingly, Paul claimed each of these points was revealed to him in that one encounter with the risen Lord Jesus.

The Gospel can be stated in these simple points, and each point is undeniably required for salvation:

- You must believe that the man, Jesus Christ, is God.
- You must believe that Jesus Christ is Lord and King.
- You must believe that the Kingdom is spiritual and for all people.
- You must believe that Christ's death and resurrection established the Kingdom.
- You must adopt God's value system.

Each of these points is essential to the Gospel and must be used to determine whether or not a person is truly a Christian. They are the sole dividing line for Christian fellowship. With them we have clear requirements for assessing whom we accept and reject as being Christ's disciples. Conversely, we also know which issues are irrelevant for determining Christian identity. Therefore, we can break down the walls of separation we have imposed based on our traditions and our interpretations of the Bible. Any ideas beyond the Gospel must never divide believers because they are only *our* traditions and interpretations, and they are not part of *God's* Gospel.

Finally, both Jesus and Paul considered a transformed life to be an identifying mark of whether or not someone was a believer. Peter, James, and John also taught that love for one another was inseparable to true faith in Christ. Ideological belief was not a sufficient test of salvation. Jesus regarded a person only to have entered his Kingdom if he had adopted the value system of the Kingdom.

2. Galatians 1:11-24

20 Jesus Is Both God and Man

The New Testament states clearly that Jesus was a real man. It emphasizes his birth, death, and years of interacting with people. Even so, the King of the Kingdom of God is no mere man. He is from God and is God.[1] Jesus performed many miracles, signs and wonders to impress this upon his hearers, even demonstrating his power over nature and spirits.

When Jesus' opponents challenged his claim of authority, they all came with differing ideas of who the Christ was.[2] However, he showed them that the true Messiah was not merely the son of David, but also the Son of God. He came not only to fulfill the promise to David, but also to sit on the throne of the Kingdom of God. Jesus is the Son of David, and he is also the divine Son, the Son of God.

Believing Jesus is God is not optional if you want to enter his Kingdom. The Kingdom is the Kingdom *of God*. Without recognizing that it is run by God, the King of the Kingdom, you cannot enter it. Jesus' place is foremost in the Kingdom because he is God.

Paul also taught that Jesus Christ is God.[3] Jesus was indeed a man

---

1. John 1:1 In the beginning was the Word, and the Word was with God, and the Word was God.

2. Matthew 22:15-46

3. Colossians 1:15-20 He is the image of the invisible God, the firstborn of all creation. For by him all things were created, in heaven and on earth, visible and invisible, whether thrones or dominions or rulers or authorities—all things were created through him and for him. And he is before all things, and in him all things hold to-

but he was, at the same time, God. He was not merely a man whom God chose to be ruler, but the Ruler himself who chose to become man.

Believing Jesus is God is an undeniable element of the Christian faith. Anyone who believes that Jesus was only a man and not God does not believe the Gospel. We must believe Jesus is God, but also a man who died on a cross.

There was no doubt in the minds of those who condemned Jesus to death that he claimed to be the Son of God. This was one of their charges against him when they sought his crucifixion.[4]

The true Church has historically never been in doubt about the humanity and divinity of Christ. This has always been a foundational truth in tradition, the early Church documents, and the Bible.

---

gether. And he is the head of the body, the church. He is the beginning, the firstborn from the dead, that in everything he might be preeminent. For in him all the fullness of God was pleased to dwell, and through him to reconcile to himself all things, whether on earth or in heaven, making peace by the blood of his cross.

4. Matthew 26:63-65 But Jesus remained silent. And the high priest said to him, "I adjure you by the living God, tell us if you are the Christ, the Son of God." Jesus said to him, "You have said so. But I tell you, from now on you will see the Son of Man seated at the right hand of Power and coming on the clouds of heaven." Then the high priest tore his robes and said, "He has uttered blasphemy. What further witnesses do we need? You have now heard his blasphemy."

21 Jesus Is Lord and King

The starting place in Jesus' teaching was his claim to be the King of a Kingdom. Everything Jesus taught hinged on that beginning element. The word "Christ" is the Greek word for the Hebrew word "Messiah," which means "anointed one." The anointed one for the Jew was the king chosen by God.

No one can enter the Kingdom of God without acknowledging that it exists and that it has a King. No one can enter the Kingdom of God without becoming a subject of the King. Without first recognizing the King, you will never recognize the Kingdom. Without first understanding the King, you will never understand the Kingdom. The two ideas are inseparable. The King always precedes the Kingdom, and the Kingdom cannot be understood apart from the King. Jesus said he is the only way to the Father because of his place as Head of the Kingdom.

Paul conveyed his recognition of Jesus Christ as King by consistently referring to him with the title "Lord." Jesus is the Lord, the Master. Paul was his slave. He used this language to demonstrate that Christ was his King.

You must accept that Christ is the King, your King, in order to be saved. Consider this very thorough language describing someone with great power and authority.

> *...[God] worked in Christ when he raised him from the dead and seated him at his right hand in the heavenly places, far above all*

> *rule and authority and power and dominion, and above every name that is named, not only in this age but also in the one to come. And he put all things under his feet and gave him as head over all things to the church...*[1]

Paul declared that Christians are not to live for themselves, but for Christ.[2] There are two aspects to no longer living for yourself. Obviously, if you have someone who is Lord over you, you must do what he commands. However, being in Christ's Kingdom is not as much about doing what he commands as it is about becoming like him. In other words, he is the King and you must adopt his value system. It is one thing to obey the rules of the King, and quite another to live for him. Living for him implies a life of devoted service. You do not obey because you *must* obey, but because you really *want* to obey.

Unless that transformation has occurred within your heart, you are not in Christ's Kingdom. Until you have sworn loving devotion to Jesus as your King, you are still living for yourself and, presumably, your own earthly kingdom. You cannot be devoted to Christ and remain devoted to serving yourself. You must bow your knee before Christ, not because you must, but because it is the deepest desire of your heart.

1. Ephesians 1:20-22

2. 2 Corinthians 5:14-15 For the love of Christ controls us, because we have concluded this: that one has died for all, therefore all have died; and he died for all, that those who live might no longer live for themselves but for him who for their sake died and was raised.

22 The Kingdom Is Spiritual

There are several crucial elements to Christ's Kingdom, and Jesus stressed each of these aspects when he described it: it is not an earthly kingdom; it takes precedence over all other kingdoms; it operates by different rules than earthly kingdoms; those in the Kingdom must seek to extend it; it operates alongside the kingdoms of this world; and the Kingdom of God is for all people. Each of these elements is a non-negotiable part of what Jesus taught about the Kingdom. Removing any one of these from your description of the Kingdom disfigures it.

The Kingdom is not an earthly kingdom

Though Jesus continuously taught his Kingdom was not of this world, it seems to be one of the most ignored doctrines about the Kingdom. Throughout history, men have sought to have the Kingdom of God on earth. This is an outright contradiction with everything Jesus did and taught. Jesus' cross is a stumbling block to Jews precisely because he did not give them an earthly kingdom.[1]

In the fourth century, when the Roman emperor Constantine claimed to have God on his side in establishing an earthly kingdom, he was clearly wrong. Anyone claiming that his establishment of an earthly kingdom is God-willed and God-directed is mistaken. Jesus'

1. 1 Corinthians 1:23 …but we preach Christ crucified, a stumbling block to Jews and folly to Gentiles…

Kingdom is emphatically not of this world.[2]

Since God's Kingdom is not of this world, it was not established as kingdoms of this world are established. It is not expanded as kingdoms of this world are expanded. It is not ruled as kingdoms of this world are ruled. Jesus clearly said, "My Kingdom is not of this world." Any time Christians seek to establish the Kingdom of God on earth, they are not following Christ; they are following their own wills and desires.

This grievous error has been made many times over the centuries by people claiming to follow Christ. Totally missing the true message of the cross, they seek to establish something Christ rejected as the temptation of Satan. Jesus chose to die on the cross rather than serve Satan by establishing an earthly kingdom.[3]

The Kingdom of God is preeminent

Even though the Kingdom is not of this world, it holds first place over everything in this world. Jesus taught all things earthly must be subordinate to his kingship and his Kingdom. This extends to everything in life: nothing is excluded. The Kingdom is more important than power, wealth, money, family, and all other human relationships. Jesus requires absolute devotion above all else.[4]

Our loyalty to the King and his Kingdom must take precedence over every other relationship. The remarkable thing about this is that once you understand the Kingdom, you realize your devotion to the King enhances, rather than hinders, your other relationships. It is by living the value system of the Kingdom that you truly learn how to live in relationship with others.

The Kingdom operates by different rules

Christ's Kingdom is not of this world, and it does not operate by the rules of this world. It is not run by men, and it does not operate like the kingdoms of men. The laws of Christ's Kingdom are funda-

2. John 18:36 Jesus answered [Pilate], "My kingdom is not of this world. If my kingdom were of this world, my servants would have been fighting, that I might not be delivered over to the Jews. But my kingdom is not from the world."

3. I am not overlooking the fact that Jesus' death was salvific. But his death demonstrates the very value system of his Kingdom and it cannot be modeled in any earthly kingdom. Jesus did not die on the cross to establish an earthly Kingdom.

4. Matthew 10:37-38 Whoever loves father or mother more than me is not worthy of me, and whoever loves son or daughter more than me is not worthy of me. And whoever does not take his cross and follow me is not worthy of me.

mentally different. The entire point of the collection of Jesus' teachings known as the Sermon on the Mount[5] is to demonstrate the value system of Christ's Kingdom. Jesus reiterated various laws that the Jews were told to live by, but then stated how different life would be in his Kingdom. The Law and rules of men do not apply in his Kingdom.

If we wish to enter the Kingdom, we must adopt the value system of the King. His ethical system is unlike any legal system used in earthly kingdoms. Christ values something different in his Kingdom than people value in their kingdoms: *Love and forgiveness are the law and the consequence in Christ's Kingdom.* The law of the Kingdom is love, and the consequence of breaking that law is receiving forgiveness.[6] This is a value system apart from anything on earth. There is no way to force the law or the consequence on unwilling people. That is why your willingness to adopt this value system is a requirement for entering the Kingdom.

Members of the Kingdom extend it

Every member of the Kingdom of God is called to help extend the Kingdom. Part of extending the Kingdom is telling others about the King and the Kingdom. Identifying the King to those outside the Kingdom is how even the least in the Kingdom is greater than John the Baptist. You cannot be in the Kingdom if you do not know who the King is, or if you are unwilling to do the work of removing mountains to prepare hearts for the King. We are all called to take up the work of John the Baptist and remove the mountains that stand in the way of people coming to the King. We are all called to point out who the King is. If the least in the Kingdom is pointing people to Christ, then those who do not point others to Christ are not in the Kingdom.

The Kingdom of God is not extended as though it were an earthly kingdom. We do not wage war or use weapons to expand Christ's Kingdom. We do not attempt to extend his Kingdom through force of any kind. Jesus did not come to promote a revolt or rebellion. Although his Kingdom transcends the kingdoms of this world, it does not eliminate them. In his discussion with the Pharisees, Jesus was presented with the issue of taxes. He supported the position that the Jews had under Roman rule, but he also pointed people to their greater obligation of serving God.

---

5. Matthew 5-7
6. Matthew 5:21-24

The Kingdom operates alongside earthly kingdoms

Jesus' answer about taxes showed he was not interested in a political kingdom. He did not come as the revolutionary leader many expected or desired. He came to establish the Kingdom of God, a spiritual Kingdom that operated alongside the kingdoms of this world. Although Jesus' Kingdom exists parallel to earthly kingdoms, his value system and the ethics of his Kingdom are intended to bleed over into earthly kingdoms. As his Kingdom expands, those with dual citizenship bring to earthly kingdoms the values they have learned in the heavenly Kingdom.

The Kingdom of God is for all people

Finally, Jesus taught his Kingdom does not extend, but supersedes the Israelite kingdom. It might be difficult for some to accept this as the teaching of Christ since there is much disagreement on this issue within the Church. But Jesus made it clear that his Kingdom was not for Jews only, but for Jews and Gentiles. He demonstrated his acceptance of Gentiles into his Kingdom on several occasions.

Anyone still in doubt must face Jesus' most significant words on this subject. Jesus' blood forms a New Covenant that *does away* with the Old Covenant. Living under the Old Covenant with its Law is no longer an option. With the establishment of Christ's Kingdom, you either live in his Kingdom or you live in rebellion to God. If we live in the Kingdom, we keep the one rule of the Kingdom. We do not need a list of rules to please God; he is pleased when we have sacrificial love for one another.

Paul's view of the Kingdom

Paul agreed with all that Jesus taught. He made no attempt to promote an earthly kingdom, and he taught believers that their obedience to Christ preceded any desires of earthly rulers. Where Christians could live peacefully alongside the Roman kingdom, they should.[7] He also encouraged them to share their faith in Christ with those around them.

Paul was forced to deal with the issue of false teachers who deceived Christians into living by the Law rather than by grace. He wrote about the Christian's freedom from the Law and his position before

7. Romans 13:1-8

God based on God's gracious action. Many opposed Paul because their concept of a person's standing before God was still influenced by their understanding of the Old Covenant rather than the New Covenant. Paul's entire letter to the Galatians concerned this.

> *We ourselves are Jews by birth and not Gentile sinners; yet we know that a person is not justified by works of the law but through faith in Jesus Christ, so we also have believed in Christ Jesus, in order to be justified by faith in Christ and not by works of the law, because by works of the law no one will be justified.*[8]

Christians do not have to follow the Old Testament Law because it does not apply to them. There is no law that a Christian must do to be saved. We will never be justified in God's sight through legalism, works, or obedience to a list of rules. None of those can save us. Paul made it clear that they have nothing to do with the Gospel. Salvation is Christ's work, not our own.

Paul was extremely opposed to advocates of the Law. He knew the danger Christians faced if they sought to live by the Law rather than through transformation in value system by the Holy Spirit. When you live by the Law, the best you can hope for is to reflect the value system of God. Where the commandment requires you to do good to another, you only reflect the glory of God when you obey it.

However, with Christ you can be transformed in your heart by adopting the value system of sacrificial love for the benefit of others. This inner change allows you to then radiate God's glory yourself. You no longer merely reflect God's goodness, you become good yourself. You are transformed into his likeness. The Law cannot and does not do that. Doing the Law can only make you look good, but adopting God's value system brings glorious transformation to goodness.

Paul also taught that the Kingdom was for all nations. Paul tended to use the word "Church" rather than "Kingdom," but his meaning was clearly the same. The Jew has no additional privilege in the Kingdom of God over a Gentile. Paul dealt with this concept in his letters to the Galatians and the Romans.

In Galatians, Paul demonstrated that the Gospel is the only means by which a Jew can be saved, and that same Gospel is the only means by which Gentiles, too, can be saved. In Romans, Paul discussed the

8. Galatians 2:15-16

advantages that Jews had in being the chosen people of God,[9] but he pointed out that none of those advantages led to salvation. Both Jew and Gentile are equally condemned and equally needing Christ as Savior.[10] Not only are they equal in those two respects, there is now no distinction between Jew and Gentile in the Kingdom.[11]

Paul also focused on one other idea: there is only one Body.[12] Jews and Gentiles are equal and united in Christ.[13] There are not two bodies, one Jew and one Gentile. There is only one Body made up of all believers, from all nations, cultures, backgrounds, and time periods. The Church is one unified whole in spite of great diversity.[14] We were all once hostile to God, but are now at peace with him. We were once hostile to each other, but are now united into one Body.[15] This is the powerful ministry of reconciliation God has done for us and given to us.[16]

Near the end of Paul's letter to the Romans, he taught one of the most significant teachings for the Church.[17] Paul instructed us to ac-

---

9. Romans 3:1-2; 9:4-5

10. Romans 3:28-30 For we hold that one is justified by faith apart from works of the law. Or is God the God of Jews only? Is he not the God of Gentiles also? Yes, of Gentiles also, since God is one. He will justify the circumcised by faith and the uncircumcised through faith.

11. Galatians 3:27-28 For as many of you as were baptized into Christ have put on Christ. There is neither Jew nor Greek, there is neither slave nor free, there is neither male nor female, for you are all one in Christ Jesus.

12. Ephesians 4:4-6 There is one body and one Spirit—just as you were called to the one hope that belongs to your call—one Lord, one faith, one baptism, one God and Father of all, who is over all and through all and in all.

13. Ephesians 3:6 This mystery is that the Gentiles are fellow heirs, members of the same body, and partakers of the promise in Christ Jesus through the gospel.

14. Colossians 3:11 Here there is not Greek and Jew, circumcised and uncircumcised, barbarian, Scythian, slave, free; but Christ is all, and in all.

Galatians 3:28 There is neither Jew nor Greek, there is neither slave nor free, there is neither male nor female, for you are all one in Christ Jesus.

15. Ephesians 2:13-14 But now in Christ Jesus you who once were far off have been brought near by the blood of Christ. For he himself is our peace, who has made us both one and has broken down in his flesh the dividing wall of hostility...

16. 2 Corinthians 5:18-19 All this is from God, who through Christ reconciled us to himself and gave us the ministry of reconciliation; that is, in Christ God was reconciling the world to himself, not counting their trespasses against them, and entrusting to us the message of reconciliation.

17. Romans 14:1-15:7

cept anyone whom God has accepted.[18] We must not reject anyone whom God has welcomed into his Kingdom. It may be easy for us to nod agreement if we only think in terms of male, female, rich, poor, slave, free, Jew, and Gentile. But we need to think in terms of everyone who believes the Gospel, even if they hold to a different Christian tradition or interpretation.

This is why it is so important to correctly understand and define the Gospel. *God accepts into his Kingdom everyone who gets the Gospel right* no matter what other traditions and interpretations they have added to their Christianity. Any tradition or interpretation that does not oppose the Gospel, though different from your traditions and interpretations, is no ground for rejecting another believer. *If Christ has accepted them, then so must you.* You have no choice. Anything short of that puts you in jeopardy of getting the Gospel wrong yourself.

The Gospel is the unifying factor of the Kingdom, the Church. It is the measure of whom we must accept as a brother or sister. Both Jesus and Paul affirmed that uniqueness of the Kingdom. It is not an earthly kingdom; it is far more than any earthly kingdom could ever be. It is a place where all people who adopt the one law of love can be accepted by other people in the way God has accepted them.

---

18. Romans 15:7 Therefore welcome one another as Christ has welcomed you, for the glory of God.

23 The Kingdom Is Established by Death and Resurrection

An essential part of the Gospel is the belief that not only has Christ been raised from the dead, but *all* those in his Kingdom will also be raised from the dead. The death and resurrection of Christ not only established his Kingdom; they are the means by which we enter it and the basis for our faith in our own resurrection.

No one can enter the Kingdom without belief in resurrection from the dead. This was a major issue of disagreement between Jesus and the Sadducees since they did not believe in a resurrection. Although developed more theologically by Paul, we cannot read the Gospel accounts without recognizing the importance of the resurrection of Christ. Not only does it provide the exclamation point to the Gospel message, it was clearly part of God's plan for the establishment of his Kingdom *from the very beginning.*

Paul summarized the Gospel with this statement: "I decided to know nothing among you except Jesus Christ and him crucified."[1] Jesus Christ was a man and he died on a cross. Paul never questioned the humanity of Jesus. We cannot be saved if we do not believe that Jesus was crucified as a man. But we also believe in a God who raises the dead.[2] This is a fundamental doctrine in Christianity. Everything we

1. 1 Corinthians 2:2

2. 2 Corinthians 1:9 Indeed, we felt that we had received the sentence of death. But that was to make us rely not on ourselves but on God who raises the dead.

do in life should hinge on our belief that life does not end with death. Resurrection is a crucial, inseparable part of the Gospel.

Resurrection life is a common idea of Paul in his letter to the Romans.[3] Abraham's faith is very important in Christian thought, and we are called to have faith like his. Abraham's faith was tied to his belief that God gives life to the dead. He became the one through whom all nations are blessed because he believed God gives life to those who do not exist.[4]

If you do not believe in resurrection from the dead, then you cannot believe Jesus was raised from the dead. Or maybe you believe he was raised, but you do not think anyone else has or will be. Nevertheless, without belief in resurrection, Christianity is pointless.[5]

Paul also included another aspect to his belief that God raises the dead. The transformation of believers at the return of Christ negates any experience of physical death on their part.[6] This is connected to resurrection because the bodies of all believers will be transformed by God's power that raises the dead.[7]

Salvation through resurrection

Paul expanded his idea of Christ's death by describing two aspects of our relationship with God that change because of the death of Christ on the cross and his resurrection. Both of these are crucial to our entering the Kingdom.

---

2 Corinthians 4:14 ...knowing that he who raised the Lord Jesus will raise us also with Jesus and bring us with you into his presence.

3. Romans 8:11 If the Spirit of him who raised Jesus from the dead dwells in you, he who raised Christ Jesus from the dead will also give life to your mortal bodies through his Spirit who dwells in you.

4. Romans 4:16-17 That is why it depends on faith, in order that the promise may rest on grace and be guaranteed to all his offspring—not only to the adherent of the law but also to the one who shares the faith of Abraham, who is the father of us all, as it is written, "I have made you the father of many nations"—in the presence of the God in whom he believed, who gives life to the dead and calls into existence the things that do not exist.

5. 1 Corinthians 15:13-14 But if there is no resurrection of the dead, then not even Christ has been raised. And if Christ has not been raised, then our preaching is in vain and your faith is in vain.

6. 1 Thessalonians 4:13-18

7. Philippians 3:20-21 But our citizenship is in heaven, and from it we await a Savior, the Lord Jesus Christ, who will transform our lowly body to be like his glorious body, by the power that enables him even to subject all things to himself.

First, we receive forgiveness of our sins through Christ's sacrificial death on the cross.[8] Christ's one sacrifice completely and forever solves the problem of the penalty for choosing our own value systems. Second, we are justified by Christ's resurrection.[9] This idea is not fully developed in the Gospels, but righteousness by faith is stressed thoroughly by Paul. Although Jesus taught his Kingdom was established through death and resurrection, Paul broke it down into two parts to demonstrate what God was doing in our salvation. We are restored to right relationship with God, not through keeping the Law,[10] but through the death of Christ as a man under the Law.[11]

In justification, the righteousness of Christ is credited to us while our sin is transferred to Christ on the cross. The Son received the curse of God when the Father turned his back on him because of our rebellion. Christ paid the penalty for our value systems while giving us his righteousness (the effect of his obedience to God's value system). When God looks at us, he does not measure our relationship with him by how well we do his value system, but by his relationship with Jesus.

From a relational standpoint, he regards us as though we are as righteous as Christ. In other words, he treats us as though we perfectly share and do *his* value system.[12] This is essential, for we must be as righteous as God—the highest standard of righteousness—to enter heaven. You will never attain it on your own, because having sacrificial love like Jesus is more difficult for us than walking on water.

---

8. Ephesians 1:7 In him we have redemption through his blood, the forgiveness of our trespasses, according to the riches of his grace...

Colossians 2:13-14 And you, who were dead in your trespasses and the uncircumcision of your flesh, God made alive together with him, having forgiven us all our trespasses, by canceling the record of debt that stood against us with its legal demands. This he set aside, nailing it to the cross.

9. Romans 4:24-25 It will be counted to us who believe in him who raised from the dead Jesus our Lord, who was delivered up for our trespasses and raised for our justification.

2 Corinthians 5:21 For our sake he made him to be sin who knew no sin, so that in him we might become the righteousness of God.

10. Galatians 2:16 ...yet we know that a person is not justified by works of the law but through faith in Jesus Christ, so we also have believed in Christ Jesus, in order to be justified by faith in Christ and not by works of the law, because by works of the law no one will be justified.

11. Galatians 3:13 Christ redeemed us from the curse of the law by becoming a curse for us—for it is written, "Cursed is everyone who is hanged on a tree"...

12. See Appendix: Justification, Sanctification, and Glorification

Justification comes as a gift, not through law or works or any other action on our part.[13] It is God's gracious gift to all those who seek to enter his Kingdom. We are justified not only because of the cross, but also because of Christ's resurrection; it is a crucial part in our justification. In his resurrection from the dead, Jesus forever demonstrated he could keep his promises to us. His resurrection proves his promise to resurrect us is true.

Christ's resurrection allows him to stand before God as our King Representative, and empowers our faith to live a sacrificial life. Your sacrifice in this life demonstrates to you and others how deeply you believe in resurrection.[14] Only those who deeply believe in resurrection life will have the faith to offer themselves in sacrificial love for others.

The extension of Christ's Kingdom is work done by faith because we do it even though it requires suffering and death. Without faith in a God who raises the dead, it makes no sense to give up your life for others and God. If we believe this life is all we have, then we might choose to use it only for self and not others. However, we believe sacrificial service is rewarded, and that even death will not keep us from God.[15]

---

13. Romans 3:21-26 But now the righteousness of God has been manifested apart from the law, although the Law and the Prophets bear witness to it—the righteousness of God through faith in Jesus Christ for all who believe. For there is no distinction: for all have sinned and fall short of the glory of God, and are justified by his grace as a gift, through the redemption that is in Christ Jesus, whom God put forward as a propitiation by his blood, to be received by faith. This was to show God's righteousness, because in his divine forbearance he had passed over former sins. It was to show his righteousness at the present time, so that he might be just and the justifier of the one who has faith in Jesus.

14. Philippians 3:8-9 Indeed, I count everything as loss because of the surpassing worth of knowing Christ Jesus my Lord. For his sake I have suffered the loss of all things and count them as rubbish, in order that I may gain Christ and be found in him, not having a righteousness of my own that comes from the law, but that which comes through faith in Christ, the righteousness from God that depends on faith that I may know him and the power of his resurrection, and may share his sufferings, becoming like him in his death, that by any means possible I may attain the resurrection from the dead.

15. Matthew 16:24-27 Then Jesus told his disciples, "If anyone would come after me, let him deny himself and take up his cross and follow me. For whoever would save his life will lose it, but whoever loses his life for my sake will find it. For what will it profit a man if he gains the whole world and forfeits his life? Or what shall a man give in return for his life? For the Son of Man is going to come with his angels in the glory of his Father, and then he will repay each person according to what he has done."

24 We Must Adopt God's Value System

In the previous four chapters, I presented four doctrines we need to believe about the Kingdom in order to be in the Kingdom. We now need to consider what application of those beliefs God expects of us as evidence of salvation. Anyone who thinks that merely believing the aforementioned truths is sufficient for salvation does not yet understand the message of the Gospel. If the first part of the Gospel is what we believe, then what are the implications of that belief for our lives? What must we do as the inevitable outcome of our faith? What are the actions accompanying those beliefs?

This may seem repetitive since I have already covered this material. However, it is important to recognize that Paul was in complete agreement with what Jesus taught in terms of our reconciliation with God, our need to forgive, and our obligation to serve one another.

Reconciliation

Our reconciliation with God is demonstrated through nothing other than our adopting his value system. Jesus taught that, as a member of his Kingdom, you would love others as he does. Doing this does not *make* you part of the Kingdom; it demonstrates you *are* part of the Kingdom. We do not do what is good to get into the Kingdom; we do what is good because we have been reconciled to God. When we adopt his value system, love and righteousness will increase in our lives.[1] It is

---

1. Philippians 1:9-11 And it is my prayer that your love may abound more and

the fruit of being united with Christ.[2]

Christ's love is sacrificial for the benefit of others. That is God's value system, and it finds its ultimate expression at the cross. If we adopt his value system we will become like Christ on the cross. Jesus said that if you want to follow him you must take up your cross. He was not simply using a figure of speech; he was telling us that he requires us to have the exact same value system he had when he took up his cross.

Jesus constantly called people to adopt the value system of his Kingdom. We believe Jesus is the King and he has a Kingdom, but we must also change to be like the King in order to remain in his Kingdom.

No one enters Christ's Kingdom without first dealing with the issue of sin. Relationship with God must be restored if you will enter the Kingdom of God. Confession is acknowledging your value system does not agree with God's. Repentance is a change occurring within your heart when you realize you have been living by your own value system and now seek to adopt God's value system as your own. Repentance is moving from your value system to God's value system.

Paul taught that Christ's death allows for our reconciliation with God. All theology is relational, and the motive of God in our salvation is our reconciliation with him.[3] There is no aspect of theology that does not have its basis in the relational aspect of God.

To be reconciled with God means to adopt his value system. This is the only means by which we can be restored to fellowship with him, because relationship is based on having a common value system. Adopting God's value system means becoming like him in life—in all our actions toward God, toward others, and toward self.

God's value system includes dying for those who hate him, in order that he may restore relationship with them.[4] He died for us be-

---

more, with knowledge and all discernment, so that you may approve what is excellent, and so be pure and blameless for the day of Christ, filled with the fruit of righteousness that comes through Jesus Christ, to the glory and praise of God.

2. Colossians 3:1-17

3. 2 Corinthians 5:18-19 All this is from God, who through Christ reconciled us to himself and gave us the ministry of reconciliation; that is, in Christ God was reconciling the world to himself, not counting their trespasses against them, and entrusting to us the message of reconciliation.

4. Romans 5:8-10 ...but God shows his love for us in that while we were still sin-

fore we changed our value systems. He demonstrated his value system first, seeking to reconcile us to himself and to have us adopt his value system. Christ's death removes the penalty for our sin, allowing our relationship with God in this life to depend on Jesus as King Representative. But only those in his Kingdom receive that benefit.

Jesus taught that entering his Kingdom was an issue of value system. Many people want to enter the Kingdom, but do not want to change their value systems. They might want to be believers or avoid hell, and they might even think they are in his Kingdom; but they are still on the outside. They never entered it. *No one enters his Kingdom without adopting his value system, because that is what it means to be reconciled to God.*

Forgiveness

Not only must we be forgiven by God, we must also be as forgiving as God. We cannot be in the Kingdom if we are not willing to be forgiving. Jesus made it clear that since God is forgiving, all those who would be like God must also be forgiving.[5]

Why is forgiveness so important to God? Because God's love most looks like Jesus on the cross, and the reason Jesus went to the cross was that we might be forgiven. Forgiveness is sacrificial love for others. Forgiving someone who has sinned against you, not holding that offense against him, demonstrates how much like God you have become.

Paul also taught that you must forgive others as you have been forgiven. We forgive because Christ has forgiven us. This is a crucial part of how Paul expected believers to live. As we have experienced God's forgiveness, we are to forgive fellow believers.[6]

Forgiveness involves the confession and repentance of the sinner so that his value system changes from an unloving, offending one to

---

ners, Christ died for us. Since, therefore, we have now been justified by his blood, much more shall we be saved by him from the wrath of God. For if while we were enemies we were reconciled to God by the death of his Son, much more, now that we are reconciled, shall we be saved by his life.

5. Matthew 6:14-15 For if you forgive others their trespasses, your heavenly Father will also forgive you, but if you do not forgive others their trespasses, neither will your Father forgive your trespasses.

6. Colossians 3:12-13 Put on then, as God's chosen ones, holy and beloved, compassion, kindness, humility, meekness, and patience, bearing with one another and, if one has a complaint against another, forgiving each other; as the Lord has forgiven you, so you also must forgive.

one that serves, gives, and sacrifices. Although forgiveness is not optional for the believer, reconciliation with an offender requires his willingness to cease his selfish value system. We seek to reconcile others to God and to ourselves; however, not all will be reconciled.

Within the Kingdom there should never be an unwillingness to be reconciled since we are all seeking the same value system and the attendant relationships it affords. No one in the Kingdom should continue in sin when he has loving support to overcome it. And no one in the Kingdom should be unforgiving, since forgiveness is the very basis for his being in the Kingdom of God.

Service

Jesus also taught that greatness comes through service.[7] Service in Jesus' Kingdom contains all the facets of our sacrificial love for others. Serving one another is not optional in his Kingdom. He made it clear that he came to serve others; and, if we would be like him, we must not only be *willing* to serve others but *actually* serve them.

Paul continued Christ's teaching on love rather than Law. The freedom we have in Christ is not a freedom to live for self, but in service for others.[8] We cannot exploit others if we have Christ's value system and are in his Kingdom. This is a distinguishing mark of all who call themselves his disciples.

Sacrificial love is our calling within all our relationships, whether between husbands and wives, parents and children, or masters and slaves.[9] We are to love each other in a sacrificial way, adopting his value system. *Everything else is an application of this commandment.* In other words, when Paul told husbands, wives, parents, children, masters and slaves how they must act, he was not giving a list of rules for them to follow. He was explaining to them how sacrificial love is

7. Matthew 20:25-28 But Jesus called them to him and said, "You know that the rulers of the Gentiles lord it over them, and their great ones exercise authority over them. It shall not be so among you. But whoever would be great among you must be your servant, and whoever would be first among you must be your slave, even as the Son of Man came not to be served but to serve, and to give his life as a ransom for many."

8. Galatians 5:13-14 For you were called to freedom, brothers. Only do not use your freedom as an opportunity for the flesh, but through love serve one another. For the whole law is fulfilled in one word: "You shall love your neighbor as yourself."

9. Ephesians 5

demonstrated in those various relationships.

This summarizes all we need to be and do. We do not need law. We need sacrificial love as our guiding principle.[10] Paul always emphasized love that is self-sacrificing. The imitation of Christ is sacrificial love.[11]

We must live what we believe

Together, the part that we acknowledge and the part that we do are our *belief* in the Gospel. Together they are faith. Faith is not only what we believe or acknowledge. Unless we live, act, and do the same kind of love God has demonstrated for us, we do not believe. Real faith is willing to sacrifice and die for what it believes.

God calls us to live our lives so convinced of his promises that we freely live for others. If we believe in resurrection, we will give our lives for others. If we believe God has forgiven us, we will freely forgive others. If we believe we have been reconciled to God, then we will seek to reconcile others to God. Each time we do these, we reveal how deeply we believe the promises of God and the power of his value system. But if you do not adopt God's value system, it is because you do not believe. If you do not sacrifice, or forgive, or reconcile, it is because you do not believe.

Jesus did not come only to save you from the penalty of your sins; he came to restore your relationship with God. That relationship is based on sharing a common value system with him, and you can only have it if you adopt his values and reject your own. What we believe to be true about the Kingdom is worked out in our actions here on earth. What we believe God has done for us, we must go and do for others.

The most basic rule of the Kingdom is the value system of the Kingdom. We cannot be in the Kingdom if we refuse to have the kind of love that Jesus mandates. And he does not ask us to have a love that he himself does not have. He calls us to be like him: to sacrifice and love as he has already done. God's value system is most clearly seen at the cross. It is the greatest picture of God's value system and the clearest definition of love.

---

10. 1 Corinthians 10:24 Let no one seek his own good, but the good of his neighbor.

11. Ephesians 5:1-2 Therefore be imitators of God, as beloved children. And walk in love, as Christ loved us and gave himself up for us, a fragrant offering and sacrifice to God.

25 Summary

It should now be evident that the Gospel Paul taught is the same Gospel that Jesus taught. It is a message about a King and his Kingdom. To participate in the Kingdom you must recognize that Jesus is the living King, and you worship him by loving others in the same way that he loved you.

Everything Paul taught can be summarized in these three passages consisting of only five verses:

> *...in Christ God was reconciling the world to himself, not counting their trespasses against them, and entrusting to us the message of reconciliation.*[1]
>
> *It [righteousness] will be counted to us who believe in him who raised from the dead Jesus our Lord, who was delivered up for our trespasses and raised for our justification.*[2]
>
> *We ourselves are Jews by birth and not Gentile sinners; yet we know that a person is not justified by works of the law but through faith in Jesus Christ, so we also have believed in Christ Jesus, in order to be justified by faith in Christ and not by works of the law, because by works of the law no one will be justified.*[3]

Beyond the Gospel, Paul's writings elaborate and illustrate living the Christian life. His instruction to the churches was to explain how

---

1. 2 Corinthians 5:19
2. Romans 4:24-25
3. Galatians 2:15-16

sacrificial love would affect believers' lives, and not to provide a list of rules to follow. People often seek to please God by keeping rules, but they are never transformed. There can never be enough rules to keep people from exploiting each other while making sure they are helping each other. Christians do not need a list of rules; we need only live the second part of the Gospel.

> *For you were called to freedom, brothers. Only do not use your freedom as an opportunity for the flesh, but through love serve one another. For the whole law is fulfilled in one word: "You shall love your neighbor as yourself."*[4]

If we are in the Kingdom, we will live according to the rule of the Kingdom: sacrificial love for the benefit of others. We have experienced God's sacrificial love for us, and now we are to have that same kind of love for others.

In order to be perfectly clear, and to avoid anyone suggesting that salvation is by works, let me reiterate: We are not saved by adopting God's value system, or by doing God's value system. We are saved entirely by *God* doing his value system of sacrificial love for us. However, we demonstrate that we are reconciled to God and that we are in his Kingdom by doing his value system.

The Gospel can be stated in these simple points, and each point is undeniably required for salvation:

- You must believe that the man, Jesus Christ, is God.
- You must believe that Jesus Christ is Lord and King.
- You must believe that the Kingdom is spiritual and for all people.
- You must believe that Christ's death and resurrection established the Kingdom.
- You must adopt God's value system.

A denial of any of these five points will leave you without the Gospel of the Kingdom. I do not believe there is anything listed here that can be removed without severely compromising the Gospel. This is the bare minimum. If you remove any of those beliefs, Paul would not call your message the Gospel. But neither do I think there is anything else you need add as necessary for salvation. I do not think there is anything else you could insist a Christian must also believe in order to be saved.

---

4. Galatians 5:13-14

If the Church can regain its focus on the Gospel, there will be two beautiful results. First, we will live by the standard of unity God established. We will accept all those who agree on the Gospel, and not reject people based on their traditions and interpretations. Second, in our unity, we will practice sacrificial love as Jesus intended. We will care for the Church throughout the world; and we will also work together to extend the Kingdom of God according to the Gospel, and not according to our own ideas of what we want God's Kingdom to be.

The Gospel is very simple. There is a part that we believe and a part that we do *because* of what we believe. Together they form the Gospel of the Kingdom of God. Beyond the Gospel, we have freedom to believe our various traditions and biblical interpretations.

Part 4: Sacrificial Love Applied

26 Worship and Holiness

Paul taught that we are to worship Christ as King. In order to understand what this means, we must first understand what worship is. The book of Romans explains the Gospel as two parts. Roughly speaking, Romans 1-11 describe what we must believe, while Romans 12-16 describe what we must do because of what we believe. The beginning of the second section begins with this:

> *I appeal to you therefore, brothers, by the mercies of God, to present your bodies as a living sacrifice, holy and acceptable to God, which is your spiritual worship.*[1]

After Paul concluded his theological arguments for the Gospel, he told the Romans how the Gospel should affect their lives. Most significantly, he said that *worship of God is living a life of sacrificial love.*

Worship is living like Christ on the cross. God sacrificed for you and you must now similarly sacrifice for him. That is worship. Worship is not only what you say, or something that happens when you pray or sing songs.[2] *Worship is becoming like God.* Worship is adopting his value system of love. Quoting the prophet Isaiah, Jesus said, "This people honors me with their lips, but their heart is far from me."[3] He said this to explain that worship is not what happens with the mouth,

---

1. Romans 12:1

2. It might be useful to describe transformation as spiritual worship and singing songs as vocal worship.

3. Matthew 15:8; Isaiah 29:13

but with the heart by adopting God's value system.

Paul continued the next few chapters in Romans by elaborating on what it means to be living sacrifices and to have love for one another. What he mentioned are examples of Christian love as it is lived out. That is *application* of the Gospel. The Gospel teaches us to have God's value system of sacrificial love for others, but what it looks like in practice varies by culture and time and place. Paul exhorted the Romans to love one another and gave the examples found in the second part of his letter to train them in love.

These examples produce wisdom for learning how we, too, can become sacrificial lovers. Genuine love has identifying marks in the life of a believer.[4] Sacrificial love is the fulfillment of the law, and the practitioner of it does no wrong to his neighbor, nor does he need the Law to make him do what is good or refrain from doing evil.[5] Strong Christians are to deal gently with those who are weak (that is, those who do not have the same freedom in faith because of their different traditions and interpretations).[6] They are not to please themselves, but to consider others. They are not to argue over tradition and interpretation, but to focus on the unity we have in the Gospel.

The ultimate expression of worship is loving others as deeply as Christ loved you on the cross. Nothing can or will ever surpass that kind of love. When we change to become like Christ, our actions will be like his and we will do what pleases God rather than self.[7] Transformation by the Spirit leads a believer to love others rather than to live in a sinful manner.[8] Living sinfully is living according to a value system

---

4. Romans 12:9-21

5. Romans 15:1-3 We who are strong have an obligation to bear with the failings of the weak, and not to please ourselves. Let each of us please his neighbor for his good, to build him up. For Christ did not please himself, but as it is written, "The reproaches of those who reproached you fell on me."

6. Romans 13:8-10 Owe no one anything, except to love each other, for the one who loves another has fulfilled the law. The commandments, "You shall not commit adultery, You shall not murder, You shall not steal, You shall not covet," and any other commandment, are summed up in this word: "You shall love your neighbor as yourself." Love does no wrong to a neighbor; therefore love is the fulfilling of the law.

7. 2 Corinthians 7:1 Since we have these promises, beloved, let us cleanse ourselves from every defilement of body and spirit, bringing holiness to completion in the fear of God.

8. Galatians 5:13-14 For you were called to freedom, brothers. Only do not use your freedom as an opportunity for the flesh, but through love serve one another. For

unlike God's. You cannot claim to know God if you continue to live in rebellion against him.

Paul often used lists of negative examples by which he confirmed an aspect of love that avoids doing harm to others. The person transformed in heart does not only do what is good to his neighbor, he avoids doing evil to him as well. In one of the few times Paul used Kingdom language, he claimed that transformation away from the evil values and desires of the world was an essential part of being in Christ's Kingdom.[9]

Desires of the flesh are easily identified as actions and attitudes that seek to exploit others rather than to serve them. Exploiting others is the opposite of sacrificial love. You either serve others or have them serve you. God's value system is never exploitive. Whenever someone exploits another person it is not the Holy Spirit working through him.

Those who belong to Christ will live their lives according to the value system of Christ and produce fruit that is Christ-likeness.[10] The fruit of abiding in Christ is love that is identical to Christ's love.[11]

Immediately after writing that worship is becoming like Christ in his value system of sacrificial love, Paul wrote that transformation is distancing ourselves from the value system of the world and moving toward the value system of God.

> *Do not be conformed to this world, but be transformed by the renewal of your mind, that by testing you may discern what is the will of God, what is good and acceptable and perfect.*[12]

---

the whole law is fulfilled in one word: "You shall love your neighbor as yourself."

9. Galatians 5:15-21 But if you bite and devour one another, watch out that you are not consumed by one another. But I say, walk by the Spirit, and you will not gratify the desires of the flesh. For the desires of the flesh are against the Spirit, and the desires of the Spirit are against the flesh, for these are opposed to each other, to keep you from doing the things you want to do. But if you are led by the Spirit, you are not under the law. Now the works of the flesh are evident: sexual immorality, impurity, sensuality, idolatry, sorcery, enmity, strife, jealousy, fits of anger, rivalries, dissensions, divisions, envy, drunkenness, orgies, and things like these. I warn you, as I warned you before, that those who do such things will not inherit the kingdom of God.

10. Galatians 5:22-26 But the fruit of the Spirit is love, joy, peace, patience, kindness, goodness, faithfulness, gentleness, self-control; against such things there is no law. And those who belong to Christ Jesus have crucified the flesh with its passions and desires. If we live by the Spirit, let us also walk by the Spirit. Let us not become conceited, provoking one another, envying one another.

11. John 15:1-17

12. Romans 12:2

The person who has entered Christ's Kingdom and adopted his value system changes his relationship with the world. You cannot change your relationship with God without also changing your relationship with the world. You cannot adopt God's value system without rejecting more of the value system of the world.[13] The believer has a renewed mind that turns toward the good, pure and excellent things rather than steeping itself in that which corrupts the heart.[14]

There is an important connection between holiness and love. People fail to realize this when they start making rules in order to be holy. They automatically think of holiness in terms of what we *cannot* do and what we *must* do. They immediately think of holiness as a list of rules. This is a throwback to the Law. It is not how the New Covenant functions.

Holiness is adopting God's value system and rejecting the value system of the world. Loving others sacrificially automatically produces holiness because love focuses on doing what is good to others and avoiding what is evil.[15] Christ-like love does not need a list of rules to produce this action.

Your becoming loving, becoming like Christ, *is holiness.* The holiness God wants to produce in you is all about relationship. Holiness is being separate from the value system of the world. Being holy as God is holy means not having values like the world. The person who focuses on loving action will cease engaging in activities that exploit or harm others. When such actions are removed there is no need for laws and rules.

Sacrificial love *is* worship because it exhibits our transformation to God's value system. God defines worship as loving others as he does; it is not merely our words, songs, or offerings. We only truly worship Christ by becoming like him in our actions toward others. Holiness is the natural outcome of worship because, when we worship God, we become like him.

---

13. Galatians 6:14 But far be it from me to boast except in the cross of our Lord Jesus Christ, by which the world has been crucified to me, and I to the world.

14. Philippians 4:8 Finally, brothers, whatever is true, whatever is honorable, whatever is just, whatever is pure, whatever is lovely, whatever is commendable, if there is any excellence, if there is anything worthy of praise, think about these things.

15. 1 Thessalonians 3:12-13 ...and may the Lord make you increase and abound in love for one another and for all, as we do for you, so that he may establish your hearts blameless in holiness before our God and Father, at the coming of our Lord Jesus with all his saints.

27 Sacrificial Love in the Home

We want to practice sacrificial love, not only because we are in the Kingdom, but also because we love our families. We know we should have sacrificial love in our relationships, but we need illustration so our minds can grasp the attitudes and actions of sacrificial love. Rarely does anyone physically die for others, but daily we must sacrifice for them. What does God's value system look like in the home among those who should be living like Christ?

Paul introduced a discussion on relational interaction by calling each one to measure his or her words and actions by the name of Christ.[1] That means we do everything according to his value system. Sacrificial love is all the parts of love and relationship you can imagine or read about in the Bible. When we seek to be like Christ, every part of our interaction with one another is affected. How we speak, listen, act, and forgive—all we say and do—must be done in sacrificial love.

Sacrificial speech

We have all heard and used speech that is not sacrificial. Complaining, murmuring, whining, and arguing are all about the desire to be first and to have our own way. These all reveal a heart that wants everything done according to our desires and not the desires of others. Other speech unlike Christ's contains sarcasm, mockery, and boasting.

1. Colossians 3:17 And whatever you do, in word or deed, do everything in the name of the Lord Jesus, giving thanks to God the Father through him.

All of these are a form of judgment on others flowing from pride. They reveal a heart that is not merciful, gentle, or loving.

In the case of each of these sinful forms of speech, you can see how each one promotes self over others. Consider the list again: complaining, murmuring, whining, arguing, sarcasm, mockery, and boasting. None of these build others up, nor do they try to outdo another person in showing honor.[2]

My wife and I teach our children not to speak in a dishonoring way, even if they have first been spoken to in that manner. Responding with sinful speech demonstrates the same evil desires reside in your own heart as in the heart of the one who hurt you. In contrast, when you return good speech for evil, it reveals your willingness to love even when attacked. When you give a gentle answer to the one who is angry it reveals you care more for them than you do about your own rights.

All virtues and vices relating to speech have to do with love. Virtuous speech reveals a love that sacrifices its own desires for the sake of another. Your words are only a symptom of what is in your heart. When your speech is not good it reveals your preference to have others sacrifice for you rather than to have you sacrifice for them.

At the root of all sinful forms of speech is the desire to have your own kingdom and to have others serve you. You go on the attack or complain because you are not receiving your own desires. Your heart is so unlike Christ's that instead of using loving words to help others, you pour out destructive speech that hurts them.

Loving speech builds others up. It encourages them. It causes them to be filled with the courage to achieve. Jesus heard these words from his Father, "This is my beloved Son, with whom I am well pleased."[3] Those are powerful words of encouragement. It is no surprise that the Father spoke them again as the cross neared.[4]

Speaking the truth in love forms a solid foundation for good relationships.[5] Lying, on the other hand, destroys relationship. A relationship built on the lies of one or both people is guaranteed to fail. Lying is so destructive because the relationship is built around the pretense that you both share the same value system when, in fact, you do

2. Romans 12:10 Love one another with brotherly affection. Outdo one another in showing honor.

3. Matthew 3:17

4. Matthew 17:5

5. Ephesians 4:15; 4:25

not. *Lying seeks to have the benefits of relationship without the reality of what forms relationship.* Eventually the truth comes out and the deception is discovered. The one lied to becomes grieved because the relationship they believed was real did not really exist.

Sacrificial listening

You listen sacrificially by being attentive to what another person is saying to you. Give the other person your attention, with eyes and ears and body language. We are instructed to be quick to hear,[6] and it means more than only paying attention. It means listening with a willingness to change if the conversation concerns something you are doing wrong. Your response when someone corrects your speech, actions, or attitudes reveals your willingness to be transformed to Christ-likeness.

Sacrificial listening does not go on the offensive and attack another person if it does not like what it hears. It is not defensive, trying to excuse a selfish value system. Listen with a mind to hear what is true so you might change and become more like Christ.

Sacrificial listening also means being aware of others. Do not interrupt when someone else is talking or disrupt the conversations of others. Your ideas and words are not always the most important part of the conversation, so do not keep pushing yourself to the front of the dialogue. Be patient and let others speak. If some are waiting patiently to speak, give them an opportunity to be part of the conversation.

Sacrificial action

Sacrificial action in the home involves completing tasks that must be done. Each person in the family needs to care for the other family members. Help with your share of the chores. Do you know why you might be tempted to grumble about doing chores? The answer is simple: most people do not like doing them. But why should others do them and not you? If you allow responsibility to fall only on others, it betrays your selfish value system.

Sacrificial action also includes doing what you do not think is your responsibility. "It's not my job!" never really applies at home. Imagine a household with members who only do that which is required for themselves. The cook only makes enough food for herself. Only the

---

6. James 1:19 Know this, my beloved brothers: let every person be quick to hear, slow to speak, slow to anger…

one doing laundry has clean clothes. Financial resources are only for those who gained them. This kind of home would be horrible.

Most families have a routine that dictates who is responsible for certain chores, and assign various people to special tasks as the need arises. But that is never an excuse for not serving outside your area of responsibility. Serving *when it is not required* of you is what makes an action sacrificial. Before that point you are only doing what is expected of you.

Parents should not make the mistake of thinking they should do everything for their children and thus "model sacrificial love." You must train *them* to be sacrificial. If you do everything for your children, never making them responsible for chores, you will only train them to be selfish. They must first learn to be partners in the responsibilities of the household before they will ever learn to recognize the joy it gives others when they sacrificially act on their behalf.

Another often-overlooked area of sacrificial action is participation in an activity someone else enjoys even if you do not share the same excitement about it. Doing so cultivates love and closeness in relationship. You like it when someone takes an interest in your hobbies and that which entertains you, so you also must join in the desired activities of the ones you love. Sacrifice is what you do to bring joy to others even if it is not fully pleasant for you. And, by the way, you do not have to let anyone know that what you are doing is unpleasant!

I hate to even mention this next point as a sacrifice since it should be a joy: Make sure you spend time with your family. Develop relationship around common values, but also through time together, learning to enjoy one another. This is not something only parents need to do, but children as well, especially as they grow older. A child who habitually seeks to be away from his parents and siblings[7] may one day realize he has neglected those who ought to be his closest friends in life.

Sacrificial forgiveness

Forgiveness is what we need when we get the speaking, listening and acting wrong. We need it when someone has chosen to live by his own selfish value system and has not been sacrificial to another member of the family. Without forgiveness, family relationships are

7. This is an indication that a child may not be adopting the value system of his parents. Be watchful and discover the value systems of your child's peers.

doomed. They will eventually break down and perhaps even end.

We do not like it when someone speaks to us or treats us in a dishonoring way. We also dislike it when someone makes an ugly face at us, or when others do not help carry the load around the home, or when someone ignores us when we are trying to speak with them, or when someone constantly interrupts us when we are speaking. In each of these cases, the real problem is that someone believes he does not have to sacrifice for others, but insists that others sacrifice for him. The heart never needs training to put self first, but we all need to train ourselves to be forgiving.

Do you find it easier to forgive or to ask to be forgiven? I do not usually have trouble forgiving, but my pride makes it very difficult to ask for forgiveness. It means acknowledging something about myself I wish were not true. It means I was not living God's value system; I was not being sacrificial.

Strong family relationships

You may have seen the marriage relationship illustrated with a diagram of a triangle. God is at the top of the triangle, and on the two sides are the husband and wife. Usually this illustration has the accompanying explanation: As the two individuals grow closer to God, they grow closer to each other. That is, as they move up their respective sides of the triangle, moving closer to God at the top, the horizontal distance between the two people diminishes.

This idea is true; the relational distance between two people diminishes as they grow closer to God. However, this is often taught without a clear definition of how the two people grow closer to God. For example, if the two people in the relationship have different ideas of what it means to grow spiritually, the relationship will not progress. If either the husband or wife has a wrong idea of what it means to grow closer to God, this relationship will not develop as God intends. Neither one may actually be growing closer to God because they may not be adopting his value system.

This illustration only makes sense if we understand that growth toward God is about relationship. We grow spiritually only to the extent that we adopt God's value system. Without this understanding, the diagram has very limited benefit. The more both people grow in God's value system, the more they will grow in *each other's* value system; both relationships will be centered on the same thing. And only as both people adopt God's value system will their relationship be based on a common value system that produces excellent relationship.

We were created for relationship, and relationships only work using God's value system. Every virtue and every vice relates to the idea of sacrificial love for the benefit of others. If you are the one sacrificing, your life will be filled with virtues; but if you demand others sacrifice for you, your life will be filled with vices.

Sacrificial love in our homes cultivates beautiful, strong relationships. If each person in the relationship is more willing to serve than be served, then the home will be full of cheerful lovers. If each is willing to forgive when offended, and the offender seeks to change his value system to one of sacrificial love, then the home will be a place of peace.

28 Sacrificial Love in Ministry

On the last evening before his crucifixion, Jesus taught his disciples the importance of fruitfulness, using an illustration in which he is the Vine, his Father is the Vinedresser, and we are the branches.[1] In order to make us as fruitful as possible, the Father must prune us.

The purpose of pruning is to focus growth in the plant toward producing fruit, making the growth of the plant as useful to the vinedresser as possible. Left on its own, a branch will expend too much energy developing leaves. Unfortunately, there are many things Christians think are spiritual growth that are mere greenery.

Jesus also said the Vinedresser cuts away any branch that does not bear fruit. He referred to Judas, who would be returning with soldiers to arrest Jesus later that night. The point of fruitfulness and pruning is the same: bearing fruit is *the only proof* you are Christ's disciple.[2] Since fruitfulness is so important, we must be absolutely sure of what Jesus identified as fruit, and then make sure that we are producing it.

Fortunately, we know exactly what Jesus had in mind. He commanded his disciples to have sacrificial love for each other, laying down their lives for their friends.[3] Jesus tied being his disciple and

1. John 15:1-8

2. John 15:8 By this my Father is glorified, that you bear much fruit and so prove to be my disciples.

3. John 15:12-13 This is my commandment, that you love one another as I have loved you. Greater love has no one than this, that someone lays down his life for his friends.

bearing the fruit of sacrificial love to relationship with him when he said, "You are my friends if you do what I command you."[4] Remember, relationship is based on a common value system; to be his friend you must adopt his value system.

We need to be fruitful, and that fruitfulness is sacrificial love for the benefit of others. This is the Gospel of the Kingdom. Unfortunately, most people think of the Gospel as only what God has done for them, and not the living sacrifice God requires of those in his Kingdom. To enter the Kingdom, you must adopt the value system of the King. This is the only path to relationship with God. This is the only measure of true spirituality and relationship with God.

The Church is all about serving others

People often want to know what the Church can do for them. I frequently receive telephone calls from people asking which programs and services my church offers. Those callers are usually focused on being served and not serving. Others call asking for money or some variation of financial help. There are even people who are selfish in service! They attempt to dictate what position they will have if they should come. Churches are full of people who do not understand Christ's value system. They are in churches, but some are not in the Kingdom.

Being in the Kingdom means service for *others*, sacrificial love for *others*. How do you currently show sacrificial love to those within your church? Do you give up your time and energy to help those in need?

You are in the Kingdom to be transformed into a sacrificial lover—to be like Jesus dying on the cross. God's love for you motivated his sacrifice for you. If you want to be like him, you must be motivated by sacrificial love as well.

When Jesus spoke of fruit-bearing and love, he said it would result in joy.[5] The best way to be joyless is to be half-hearted in your love. Jesus said, "It is more blessed to give than to receive,"[6] but most of us struggle to believe it. We believe it when we give gifts to our children, but that is not the standard by which Christ measures. Sacrificial love

4. John 15:14

5. John 15:11 These things I have spoken to you, that my joy may be in you, and that your joy may be full.

6. Acts 20:35

gives more than it receives. Every time we are not willing to sacrificially give of ourselves, we reveal we do not really believe those words of Christ. It is an issue of faith.

Why do bad things happen to good people?

People perpetually criticize God for the problems in the world. They wonder how God can be loving since there is so much suffering in the world. Even Christians ask why bad things happen to good people. The answer is surprisingly simple. Bad things allow God's value system to be displayed through us.

Jesus once met a man who had been born blind.[7] The disciples asked Jesus whose sin caused the man's suffering, but Jesus told them it had nothing to do with sin. Bad things happen to good people; and when they do, it is an opportunity for others to do the work of God. When you see a person suffering or in need, Jesus expects you to see it as an opportunity to practice sacrificial love for that person.

For the blind man, it was also an opportunity for faith. As he experienced the work of God in his life, he had the possibility of being transformed. Bad things sometimes happen to people so they might come to faith in Christ by experiencing the sacrificial love of Christ's followers. Suffering must always be approached as an opportunity to bring light into the world. Bad things allow us to be transformed into sacrificial lovers by doing what we can to alleviate the suffering of others.

Find somebody to love

You now know what sacrificial love is and that you are called to have it, live it, and transform the lives of others through it. You are in the Kingdom and you want, however hesitantly, to adopt the value system of the King. Now do something so God's joy may come to you. Put your faith into action by acting out the Gospel.

Find a project into which you can pour your life. It is best to find something important to you, perhaps a cause for which God has cre-

---

7. John 9:1-5 As he passed by, he saw a man blind from birth. And his disciples asked him, "Rabbi, who sinned, this man or his parents, that he was born blind?" Jesus answered, "It was not that this man sinned, or his parents, but that the works of God might be displayed in him. We must work the works of him who sent me while it is day; night is coming, when no one can work. As long as I am in the world, I am the light of the world."

ated a loving desire in your heart. What, through your sacrifice, will make the world a better place? What ministry will promote the Gospel of the Kingdom and bring salvation to others? Let me offer a few suggestions as to how you can minister to the needs of others.

Take an active role in serving within your church or a neighboring church that needs your help. If you attend a very large church, you may find you are not serving God with the gifts he has given you. Consider using your talents and abilities in a smaller fellowship. This might allow you to use teaching or musical talents that are lying fallow.

Spend a few hours a week or month with someone who is lonely or in need of a friend. Many lives can be changed by simply demonstrating this small act of loving-kindness. Develop relationships with people and you might find yourself on the receiving end of the blessing.

If there are poor and needy people in your community, perhaps you can find ways to help them improve their lives. If you have special skills, offer them freely to help those who cannot afford your time.

Often those in full time ministry continue in spite of significant financial sacrifice. Be generous in your care for their needs and offer them special gifts that they cannot regularly afford. I have a friend who regularly purchases additional groceries in order to give them to my family. This act of love is both rare and beautiful.

We must also think of the Church around the world, and not only locally. There are Christian ministries seeking to build up and establish churches around the world. Along with supporting missionaries, be involved with ministries that train pastors in countries where pastoral education is often very costly.

The Bible specifically reminds us to care for orphans. If you cannot adopt, you can certainly help those who are adopting children. International adoption can be extremely expensive, so relieving the financial burden on those adopting is a great blessing to them.

You could also involve yourself with an orphanage. There are many Christians who have established orphanages that have constant financial needs for housing, clothing, feeding, and educating the children. Providing for children in this way, and raising them in an environment where they are exposed to the Gospel, is an investment in transforming lives.

You can also become a part of an organization that offers developmental loans so Christians in poverty can achieve financial stability. This brings permanent change to their lives and benefits their communities by creating a financial environment where pastors can be supported, resulting in additional spiritual transformation.

You must be transformed

Becoming a sacrificial lover requires that you be transformed. You cannot remain the "old you" with some new projects. You must be changed in your heart and mind to love and think like Christ. You must have your value system so completely replaced by God's that you live and breathe the life of Christ.

Your life is filled with old ways of thinking and habits you have formed according to your selfish values. You have found many ways to please yourself with your time, energy, and wealth. God provides solutions for changing the parts of you that are not like him. Christians expend tremendous amounts of energy attempting to stop doing sinful deeds, but the Holy Spirit does not seek to merely break these selfish habits; he intends to replace them with sacrificial love. In fact, all sinful habits can be overcome by becoming a sacrificial lover. Where you once sought pleasure in serving self, you will now find joy in serving Christ and others.[8]

All truly sinful habits will be changed in your heart by a faith that believes God will empower you to love others as he does. The power comes not from your own will, for it is the power of the Holy Spirit of God. You provide the desire and willingness to change, and he provides the power needed to transform you. The primary reason we do not change is our hesitancy to become sacrificial lovers.

Change and fruitfulness always accompany each other. The pruning of our lives happens as we remove our selfish values and replace them with God's values. When we live our lives in sacrificial love, we find ourselves free from the entanglements of sin and become filled with the joy that comes from being like Christ.

---

8. This replacing is demonstrated in Ephesians 4:25-29. Falsehood is replaced with truthfulness; sinful anger is replaced with promptly dealing with problems; stealing is replaced with work and giving; and corrupt speech is replaced with speech that builds others up.

Avoiding the other extreme

Before you think I am suggesting we give away all our possessions and become destitute, let me clarify by using the Apostle Paul's position on this matter.[9] He taught that as we cared for one another within the Body of Christ, we were not intended to impoverish ourselves in the process.[10]

Consider Paul's wonder at the giving by Macedonian churches. Even though they were experiencing extreme poverty, they gave generously.[11] Paul did not expect this of them, nor did he command it. Their hearts were transformed to a Christ-like love that went beyond what any man would expect. This transformation of the Spirit in them even amazed Paul, a man who had given much in sacrificial love for others. God expects us to give, yet we who have plenty rarely give to an extent anyone should fear our becoming poor in the process. Live a life that will amaze those around you and compel them to live the Gospel more faithfully.

Beware of Judas

In teaching sacrificial love to his disciples, Christ gave a very important caution. On the same night he was betrayed by Judas, Jesus taught his disciples to have love for each other.[12] He stressed that the true mark of discipleship was sacrificial love, with each laying down his life for the other. But love like this is primarily for those who believe the Gospel.

Jesus taught his disciples to love sacrificially that night, but only

---

9. 2 Corinthians 8:13-14 I do not mean that others should be eased and you burdened, but that as a matter of fairness your abundance at the present time should supply their need, so that their abundance may supply your need, that there may be fairness.

10. Note that even Jesus and his disciples possessed more wealth than was necessary for their daily needs. They were not destitute, but neither were they considered rich (see Appendix: Jesus' Finances).

11. 2 Corinthians 8:1-5 We want you to know, brothers, about the grace of God that has been given among the churches of Macedonia, for in a severe test of affliction, their abundance of joy and their extreme poverty have overflowed in a wealth of generosity on their part. For they gave according to their means, as I can testify, and beyond their means, of their own free will, begging us earnestly for the favor of taking part in the relief of the saints—and this, not as we expected, but they gave themselves first to the Lord and then by the will of God to us.

12. John 13-17

after Judas left. Judas was excluded as one for whom they should lay down their lives. We are not obligated to sacrificially love those outside the Kingdom. Jesus laid down his life for his sheep, but Jesus did not die for Judas. Because Judas refused to conform to the value system of God, he exempted himself from the same love the disciples shared for one another.

This does not mean we cannot and should not have sacrificial love for those who do not believe the Gospel of the Kingdom. However, we must be very wise when we do. Those who do not share God's value system may try to exploit our love.

We must remember Jesus intends for us to put other believers *first* in our sacrificial love, and those outside the fellowship second. Again, this reveals the importance of making sure we correctly understand the Gospel and know who truly believes and who does not. Even as Judas exploited Christ, churches contain many people who seek to exploit Jesus and his followers. Some only want a free ticket to heaven. Others use Christianity as a means to a business, political, or social end. They try to exploit Jesus, and they try to exploit you.

Exploitation of others is the value system of the world. It sees another person and, instead of wanting to serve, it attempts to fulfill its own desires. That is why you must be cautious in sacrificial love. Jesus knew that his disciples, trained in sacrificial love, would always be in danger of exploitation. So he narrowed the scope of this love to those who genuinely followed him.

Christ's disciples must always seek to sacrificially love all other true disciples that share God's value system. However, the disciples were not required to have this same kind of love for Judas, lest Judas attempt to take advantage of them even as he had Christ. If Judas would betray the master for money, what would stop him from turning over others to the authorities?

You can easily measure how much a person is like Christ by the level of sacrificial love they demonstrate. Their actions will always identify them. The person who claims to follow Christ, yet takes advantage of others by exploiting them, is no disciple; he is a Judas. Jesus earnestly sought for Judas to adopt his value system. Since Judas was unwilling to change, he had to be removed that night for the protection of the true disciples.

As Christians, we view and maintain relationships based on God's love. As people with God's value system, we abhor the idea of exploiting others. Exploitation is anything that uses others for our benefit and their loss. It is the opposite of sacrificial love.

Christians must never use people. Many considered "successful" in this world have used others for their own gain.[13] Unlike them, we must care for others, especially those in need. We are to care for those who are suffering or sick. We are to care for widows and orphans and avoid the selfish stain of the world that turns its back on them.[14]

We also must care for those in our families. When people call my church asking for financial help, I inquire if they have first asked their own families and friends for help.[15] Those closest to the person have an obligation to help, but they are also most able to discern what kind of help is truly necessary. Some people do not need to be given money, and their friends and family are well aware of this. Love helps others get back on their feet; it does not enable them to maintain a sinful, exploitive value system.

Peter the shepherd

After Judas left, Jesus told his disciples that where he was going, they could not come.[16] They would follow later, but not now. Peter focused on Jesus' departure and wanted to know where Jesus was go-

---

13. James 5:4 Behold, the wages of the laborers who mowed your fields, which you kept back by fraud, are crying out against you, and the cries of the harvesters have reached the ears of the Lord of hosts.

14. James 1:27 Religion that is pure and undefiled before God and the Father is this: to visit orphans and widows in their affliction, and to keep oneself unstained from the world.

15. 1 Timothy 5:8 But if anyone does not provide for his relatives, and especially for members of his household, he has denied the faith and is worse than an unbeliever.

16. John 13:31-38 When he had gone out, Jesus said, "Now is the Son of Man glorified, and God is glorified in him. If God is glorified in him, God will also glorify him in himself, and glorify him at once. Little children, yet a little while I am with you. You will seek me, and just as I said to the Jews, so now I also say to you, 'Where I am going you cannot come.' A new commandment I give to you, that you love one another: just as I have loved you, you also are to love one another. By this all people will know that you are my disciples, if you have love for one another." Simon Peter said to him, "Lord, where are you going?" Jesus answered him, "Where I am going you cannot follow me now, but you will follow afterward." Peter said to him, "Lord, why can I not follow you now? I will lay down my life for you." Jesus answered, "Will you lay down your life for me? Truly, truly, I say to you, the rooster will not crow till you have denied me three times."

ing and why he could not follow him now. Perhaps sensing the danger, Peter stressed his willingness to sacrifice himself for Jesus. He claimed to possess sacrificial love by saying, "I will lay down my life for you."

Interestingly, Peter attempted to use Jesus' own words against him, claiming the same kind of love as the Good Shepherd.[17] Previously, Jesus said he was the Good Shepherd who lays down his life for the sheep. Peter, wanting Jesus to see his level of commitment, declared he would lay down his life for Jesus. By claiming he was willing to sacrifice himself, he wanted Jesus to know he had adopted his value system. But he had not.

We know this because, as Jesus prophesied, Peter denied his relationship with Jesus three times that very night. Peter failed at sacrificial love because sacrificial love for others is very difficult, even sacrificial love for Jesus. Once danger came, Peter's self-love and self-preservation overpowered his commitment to Christ. He learned his love for Jesus was not nearly as strong as he thought it was.

We all fail at sacrificial love. It sounds so easy, and we think we can do it, but it is very difficult. We are so easily offended, so easily distracted, and so willing to deny Christ by our actions. Every time we refuse to have sacrificial love for the Body of Christ, we deny Jesus.[18] We reject his value system and refuse his call to the new commandment to love each another.

After Christ's resurrection, he met with his disciples on a beach and fed them breakfast. There, on the shores of Galilee, Jesus asked Peter if he still thought he loved Jesus more than the others did.[19] Pe-

---

17. John 10:11 I am the good shepherd. The good shepherd lays down his life for the sheep.

18. Matthew 25:41-45 Then he will say to those on his left, 'Depart from me, you cursed, into the eternal fire prepared for the devil and his angels. For I was hungry and you gave me no food, I was thirsty and you gave me no drink, I was a stranger and you did not welcome me, naked and you did not clothe me, sick and in prison and you did not visit me.' Then they also will answer, saying, 'Lord, when did we see you hungry or thirsty or a stranger or naked or sick or in prison, and did not minister to you?' Then he will answer them, saying, 'Truly, I say to you, as you did not do it to one of the least of these, you did not do it to me.'

19. John 21:15 When they had finished breakfast, Jesus said to Simon Peter, "Simon, son of John, do you love me more than these?" He said to him, "Yes, Lord; you know that I love you." He said to him, "Feed my lambs." He said to him a second time, "Simon, son of John, do you love me?" He said to him, "Yes, Lord; you know that I love you." He said to him, "Tend my sheep." He said to him the third time, "Simon, son of John, do you love me?" Peter was grieved because he said to him the third time, "Do

ter now had a whole new understanding of the difficulty of sacrificial love. As they spoke, Jesus asked Peter three times if he loved him. Of course, the three times were intended to counteract the three denials. However, the most important point of this story is often lost.

This passage is not merely about restoring Peter after his sin. It is about how Peter could become a shepherd like the Good Shepherd. It is about Peter being transformed into the likeness of Christ by adopting Christ's value system.

Our clue to what was foremost in Jesus' mind was his telling Peter to care for his sheep. Earlier, Peter told Jesus he had "good shepherd" love. He told Jesus he could lay down his life for him. Now Jesus was holding Peter to those words. If Peter were to take the words of the Good Shepherd, he would be required to care for a flock even though it required laying down his life. Jesus wanted Peter to know that showing love for him required more than a willingness to lay down his life for Jesus: he had to be willing to lay it down *for the sheep*. To be like Christ is to sacrifice for all others in the Kingdom—not only for Christ.

Jesus then prophesied that Peter would suffer sacrificially as a shepherd, and tradition records Peter following Christ in death. We, like Peter, will not always be successful in sacrificial love. It is very difficult. Fortunately, even when we fail, Jesus never lets us go. He never gives up on those who seek to change and become like him. He continues working with us to make us effective servants. His greatest desire for us is that we live the value system we say we have adopted.

When Jesus calls us with the command, "Follow me," it is always a call to sacrificial love. The way you demonstrate your love for Christ is how you love his sheep. That is the Gospel.

---

you love me?" and he said to him, "Lord, you know everything; you know that I love you." Jesus said to him, "Feed my sheep."

29 Prayer and Sacrificial Love

Many struggle in their faith, or even reject Christianity, because they consider unanswered prayer to be an unfulfilled promise of God. If God cannot be trusted to keep his promises for the small things, how can he be trusted in the big ones? Once people begin to doubt God's word they refuse to become sacrificial lovers, because great faith is required to walk where Jesus walked.

I am convinced several "prayer promise" passages in the Bible have been seriously misinterpreted, resulting in destroyed faith and a distrust of God. To remedy this situation, we must understand what Jesus really taught about prayer; then we will not accuse God of failing to keep his promises when we think he is not answering our prayers. A correct understanding of his words will bolster faith and strengthen the Church in her mission.

The prayer promises of God most misunderstood occur in three books of the New Testament.[1] First, there are two places in Matthew referring to faith that moves mountains. Second, there are three places in John where we are told to ask whatever we wish and it will be done. And third, ideas from John are discussed again in 1 John. The passages teach us that prayer removes obstacles to entering the Kingdom, prayer empowers us to be sacrificial lovers, and prayer empowers us to love and forgive.

1. The sections addressed in this chapter require understanding extended portions of the Bible. It may be easier to follow my explanation by reading this chapter with your Bible open to the referenced texts.

Prayer removes obstacles to entering the Kingdom

The two promises in Matthew both occur in passages relating to the work of John the Baptist. According to these texts, prayer removes obstacles to people's acceptance of the King. In other words, prayer helps to prepare hearts for Christ. If you fail to see the connection with John the Baptist, you will not relate his work of moving mountains to understanding the promise. Since I have previously discussed these two texts, I will only summarize them now.

Matthew 17:20

> *He said to them, "Because of your little faith. For truly, I say to you, if you have faith like a grain of mustard seed, you will say to this mountain, 'Move from here to there,' and it will move, and nothing will be impossible for you."*

In Matthew 17, Jesus encouraged his disciples to have faith that would move mountains so they would be successful in taking up the work of John the Baptist.[2] This had nothing to do with literal mountains any more than John the Baptist moved literal mountains. Without faith, the disciples would be unable to carry on the work of John the Baptist, which was restoring people to the Father by means of pointing them to Christ. The promise in this text has nothing to do with literal mountains, nor is it a general promise to answered prayer. It refers to the specific role of the child of the Kingdom continuing the work of John in removing mountains of unbelief in hearts and restoring people to God.

Matthew 21:21-22

> *And Jesus answered them, "Truly, I say to you, if you have faith and do not doubt, you will not only do what has been done to the fig tree, but even if you say to this mountain, 'Be taken up and thrown into the sea,' it will happen. And whatever you ask in prayer, you will receive, if you have faith."*

In Matthew 21:21-22, we again have a promise regarding the moving of a mountain, and again it appears within the context of the ministry of John the Baptist.[3] The repetition of "mountain" should serve as a clue in interpreting the text. The cursing of the fig tree illustrat-

---

2. See Chapter 13: Faith Moves Mountains
3. See Chapter 15: The King Revealed

ed God's judgment against those who bore no spiritual fruit and had no likeness to God. Unless they repented and had the mountains removed, they would be cursed like the fig tree.

Even as the authorities rejected the work of John the Baptist and did not accept him as a prophet from God, they also were rejecting Jesus. People only have two options: accept the removal of mountains and prepare your heart for the King, or reject the King and be cursed. The religious authorities were cursed because they would not have the mountain moved. The prayer of faith is the means by which mountains are removed so that hearts will accept the King.

Prayer empowers us to be sacrificial lovers

In John 13-16, Jesus gave final instructions to his disciples before going to the cross. He was preparing his loved ones for the ministry they would be taking up in his stead. When this entire section of John 13-17 is read and understood as one complete unit, its teaching becomes clear.

The three prayer promise texts in John 14-16 all revolve around one sustained theme: Christ offers God's help for our becoming sacrificial lovers. He promises to truly transform us to love as he does, but only if we truly desire it and ask him for it. When we desire to have sacrificial love for others, God hears and answers.

John 14:12-14

> *Truly, truly, I say to you, whoever believes in me will also do the works that I do; and greater works than these will he do, because I am going to the Father. Whatever you ask in my name, this I will do, that the Father may be glorified in the Son. If you ask me anything in my name, I will do it.*

In John 14:14, Christ promises to do anything we ask in his name. Since no believer receives *everything* he ever asks of God, there must be more to this promise than what first appears. To fully understand what Jesus meant, we must examine the context of this promise.

Immediately prior to this promise, the disciples asked Jesus to show them the Father.[4] Jesus said that to see him *is* to see the Father,[5]

4. John 14:8 Philip said to him, "Lord, show us the Father, and it is enough for us."

5. John 14:9-11 Jesus said to him, "Have I been with you so long, and you still do not know me, Philip? Whoever has seen me has seen the Father. How can you say, 'Show us the Father'? Do you not believe that I am in the Father and the Father is in

not only because they are one, but also because they perfectly share the same value system. There is nothing Jesus would do that the Father would not do.

Then Jesus said that whoever believes in him would do greater works than even he did.[6] We share God's likeness (his value system) if we do the works of the Father as Jesus did. Understanding the prayer promise requires that we first know what the works of the Father are. So what exactly are the works Jesus has in mind?

If we move to the verse *after* the promise, we get the answer. Jesus said, "If you love me, you will keep my commandments."[7] The work of the Father is keeping Christ's commandments, and foremost is his command that we love one another.[8]

Knowing the Father and being like him comes from loving like Christ. We know God and do his work by becoming sacrificial lovers through adopting his value system. The promise regards asking God to empower us to be sacrificial lovers as Christ was. It is a promise from God to answer the prayer to be like him in this world. Anyone who sincerely prays to do the work of Christ will receive power from God to give his life in sacrificial love for others.

Prayer "in Jesus' name" is a request to be transformed into his likeness. It is not a magic phrase to connect our call to God.[9] It is our being like him in this world, and bearing his name through that which we do.

When we do the works of God in this world, it is a greater miracle than when Christ does them. When Jesus exhibits sacrificial love, it flows from his perfect value system. It is unhindered by any sin. But when we have sacrificial love, it is evidence of the work of the Holy Spirit in our lives. It takes a greater work of God to have us live in sacrificial love than for him to live in sacrificial love.

---

me? The words that I say to you I do not speak on my own authority, but the Father who dwells in me does his works. Believe me that I am in the Father and the Father is in me, or else believe on account of the works themselves.

6. John 14:12

7. John 14:15

8. John 13:34-35 A new commandment I give to you, that you love one another: just as I have loved you, you also are to love one another. By this all people will know that you are my disciples, if you have love for one another.

9. This idea is similar to the one in the Canaanite woman's prayer (see Chapter 11: A Kingdom for Everyone).

John 15:7

> *If you abide in me, and my words abide in you, ask whatever you wish, and it will be done for you.*

John 15 begins with a discussion of our need to abide in Christ and bear fruit that looks like him.[10] The fruit Jesus had in mind is discussed after the promise of John 15:7. Loving one another as Christ loved us is the fruit expected of us.[11] That love is then expressed as sacrificial love for one another: "Greater love has no one than this, that someone lays down his life for his friends."[12] So again, the abiding we are expected to do, which is tied to our asking, is our sacrificial love for the benefit of others. When we pray to love one another as Christ has loved us, God will answer our prayer by transforming us into his likeness and granting us his value system.

John 16:23-24

> *In that day you will ask nothing of me. Truly, truly, I say to you, whatever you ask of the Father in my name, he will give it to you. Until now you have asked nothing in my name. Ask, and you will receive, that your joy may be full.*

In this prayer promise, Jesus taught his disciples that they would have full access to the Father. This access comes through the Holy Spirit[13] and through the full establishment of the Kingdom at Jesus' death.[14] This text does not add a promise to the two already covered, but addresses the *means* by which the disciples' asking would change with the ascension of Christ.

With the death, resurrection, and ascension of Christ, believers gain a new freedom in approaching the Father. The disciples had a special earthly relationship with Jesus; but, until Christ became their King Representative through his death and resurrection,[15] access to the

10. See Chapter 28: Sacrificial Love in Ministry

11. John 15:9-12 As the Father has loved me, so have I loved you. Abide in my love. If you keep my commandments, you will abide in my love, just as I have kept my Father's commandments and abide in his love. These things I have spoken to you, that my joy may be in you, and that your joy may be full. This is my commandment, that you love one another as I have loved you.

12. John 15:13

13. John 16:7-15

14. John 16:16-22

15. See Appendix: Justification, Sanctification, and Glorification

Holy Spirit and the Father were both limited. Now, when we enter the Kingdom of God, the limitations are removed because the Father's relationship with us is not based on our value systems, but on the value system of Christ.

Thus, the means by which we now approach and have relationship with the Father have changed. However, the nature of our requests to him still must be within the realm of Jesus' name, which relates to our transformation into his likeness in this life.

Since the teaching in John 13-16 involves our having sacrificial love for others, loving like Christ, and becoming like him, why would we think the prayer promises have to do with anything other than our praying to become sacrificial lovers? The promises are best understood and believed if they are related to the context in which they are given: God promises to transform us into sacrificial lovers.

However, our examination of John 13-17 is not yet complete. Jesus concluded his teaching that night by praying to his Father, asking for unity among all those who would believe—a unity we are to have within the realm of God's love.[16] Those in Jesus' Kingdom have entered into the love the Father and Son share, and that same love is to be in us. Jesus referred to a common love as the basis of relationship. We are to have the same loving value system as God the Father and God the Son, for that is the only way we can have union with God.

Prayer empowers us to love and forgive

In many respects, 1 John can be considered a commentary or sermon on John 13-16. Thus, the prayer promises in 1 John make exactly the same point as in the Gospel of John.

1 John 3:22

In 1 John 3, the focus is on our being the children of God and bearing his likeness, as evidenced through our love for others. The kind of love that distinguishes us as children of God is love that lays down its life for fellow believers.[17] In other words, it is love that looks like Jesus on the cross.

It is this love that proves to us that we bear the image and likeness of God, taking away all our doubts as to whether or not we are his chil-

16. John 17:20-23

17. 1 John 3:16 By this we know love, that he laid down his life for us, and we ought to lay down our lives for the brothers.

dren.[18] We have confidence that we truly know him because we are like him, as demonstrated through sharing his value system.

The promise given in 1 John 3:22 is to receive whatever we ask from him, but the receiving is based on our keeping his commandment of love.

> *...and whatever we ask we receive from him, because we keep his commandments and do what pleases him.*

The use of the word "abide" in 1 John 3 is intended to remind us of John 15. In fact, abiding and loving are united in both texts so strongly that we cannot do justice to 1 John if we do not see it as a reflection of John 15.

Whoever abides does not ask God for selfish requests, but asks for enablement to obey the commandment to love. The love described in this chapter is an active love.[19] Love that does not act in sacrificial love is evidence of a closed heart.[20] Sharing a love like God's is the means by which we have confidence to come before God without hearts that condemn us. We must become sacrificial lovers, especially to other believers; if we do not, we may doubt God's acceptance of us.

1 John 5:15

Leading up to the final passage containing a seemingly broad prayer promise, we read that love for the Father and love for the Father's children are inseparable.[21] No one can say he loves the Father unless he also loves the Father's children. This is abiding in Christ, and it is proof of our eternal life. From John 15 and 1 John 3, we understand abiding in Christ is sharing his value system and actively loving others sacrificially.

As for the promise itself, it clearly refers to our doing the will of the Father; a will that we know requires loving one another as he has loved us.

---

18. 1 John 3:17-24

19. 1 John 3:18 Little children, let us not love in word or talk but in deed and in truth.

20. 1 John 3:17 But if anyone has the world's goods and sees his brother in need, yet closes his heart against him, how does God's love abide in him?

21. 1 John 5:1-2 Everyone who believes that Jesus is the Christ has been born of God, and everyone who loves the Father loves whomever has been born of him. By this we know that we love the children of God, when we love God and obey his commandments.

> *And if we know that he hears us in whatever we ask, we know that we have the requests that we have asked of him.*[22]

This becomes clearer once we see the verses following the promise since they explain the context of this kind of prayer. Two situations are given regarding people: one for which we pray, and one for which we do not pray.[23]

The first circumstance pertains to someone who has sinned and requires forgiveness. Jesus taught his disciples, "If you forgive the sins of anyone, they are forgiven; if you withhold forgiveness from anyone, it is withheld."[24] As we have already learned about forgiveness,[25] we are most like God when we forgive. Like John, James also ties forgiveness and prayer for the sick together.[26]

John's teaching on prayer continues on in the theme of how we must relate to one another in love, but the context of our prayer for one another is centered on confessing sins, repenting, and forgiving one another. Sacrificial love most looks like Jesus dying on the cross; so, when we love others through forgiveness, we most look like him.

The prayer God promises to answer in John 5:15 involves asking God to forgive those who repent, and healing the sinner who has been suffering physically because of sin.[27]

Jesus in the Garden of Gethsemane

In the Garden of Gethsemane, Jesus' time of prayer is contrasted with the disciples' failure at prayer.[28] In order to fully understand what Jesus believed about prayer, we must look at his prayer to the Father

---

22. John 5:15

23. 1 John 5:16 If anyone sees his brother committing a sin not leading to death, he shall ask, and God will give him life—to those who commit sins that do not lead to death. There is sin that leads to death; I do not say that one should pray for that.

24. John 20:23

25. See Chapter 4: Restoring Relationship

26. James 5:14-16 Is anyone among you sick? Let him call for the elders of the church, and let them pray over him, anointing him with oil in the name of the Lord. And the prayer of faith will save the one who is sick, and the Lord will raise him up. And if he has committed sins, he will be forgiven. Therefore, confess your sins to one another and pray for one another, that you may be healed. The prayer of a righteous person has great power as it is working.

27. Life and death in 1 John 5:16-17 refer to the result of sickness in the physical body because of sin.

28. Matthew 26:36-44 (see Chapter 17: The Rejection of the King)

that final night before his crucifixion. The last thing Jesus did before pouring himself out in sacrificial love was to spend an extended time in prayer with his Father. *Prayer was Jesus' preparation for sacrifice.*

Sacrificial love for others is not easy, and Jesus was about to face the greatest and most troubling sacrifice in the history of man. His sacrifice far outweighs any of our own, and yet even for us, sacrifice does not come easily. We struggle against the flesh, our sinful habits, and our love of self in ways Jesus did not. He was facing wrath and separation from his Father, whereas our fight is one of seeking to become like him.

Prayer is not about fulfilling our desires.[29] Jesus did not *desire* to be separated from his Father and die on the cross. His request to have the cup pass[30] was not granted, for there was no other way to save us. Jesus was not delivered from the cross; he was delivered up for others. Prayer prepared him to do the Father's will; it was not a means of avoiding it. Through prayer, we gain strength from the Father to live lives of sacrifice for others. He empowers us to reject our desires and embrace his will.

This is why the disciples failed in their commitment to Christ that night. Jesus specifically told them they needed to pray for strength to overcome the temptation to live for self.[31] They all abandoned Christ that night to preserve themselves because they were not prepared to sacrifice for his sake.

Prayer is not for receiving our desires or achieving our own will. The primary purpose of prayer is to prepare us for sacrificial living.[32] Prayer is an integral part of the process by which we adopt God's value system. He intends that we first desire to be like him before transformation occurs. Unless we freely and willingly ask the Father to transform us by the work of the Holy Spirit, we will not be transformed.

Our spiritual lives begin with the removal of obstacles standing

---

29. Unless, of course, the desire is to become a sacrificial lover!

30. Matthew 26:39 And going a little farther he fell on his face and prayed, saying, "My Father, if it be possible, let this cup pass from me; nevertheless, not as I will, but as you will."

31. Matthew 26:41 Watch and pray that you may not enter into temptation. The spirit indeed is willing, but the flesh is weak.

32. Although preparation for sacrificial love is the primary purpose of prayer, it is not the sole purpose. Though prayer has other purposes, and can be done for other reasons, we must first understand its role in love.

between the King and us. Once we come to the King, we can seek his strength to live his value system in spite of the weakness of our flesh. If we truly want to live sacrificial lives for the benefit of others, we must have faith in God's promise to transform us into his glorious likeness.

Now we have a full circle: We come to the King because someone has prayed for us and worked to remove the obstacles to our coming to the King. And once we come to the King and enter his Kingdom, we become transformed so we might pray and become the movers of mountains for others that they, too, may enter the Kingdom.

The promises God makes, he keeps. False ideas of what he has promised lead to disillusionment and destroy faith. A correct understanding of these promises guides us to prayer that transforms. Once we begin looking for the right answers to our prayers, the transformation to Christ-likeness in our lives and the lives of others produces faith. We grow in our faith as we see the work of God in our own lives and the lives of others. The prayers God accepts and answers are those for becoming a sacrificial lover. If this is your desire, God will grant it; he will give you the power to bear fruit and abide in Christ.

30 Evangelism and Value System

Before we can begin examining evangelism, we must first understand what it is. The Greek word "evangel," from which we derive the word evangelism, is translated "Gospel" in the New Testament. Gospel means "good news," therefore, evangelism is telling people the good news about the Kingdom of God.

We need to remember that when we say "Gospel" we are really shortening what Jesus said. He said it was the *Gospel of the Kingdom of God*. The good news is good news about a Kingdom. We make a sad mistake by leaving the Kingdom out of the Gospel. The reason it is such good news is that it is *God's Kingdom*. Any attempt in telling people about the Gospel must be focused on God's Kingdom.

There are many different methods of evangelism. Some preach hellfire and brimstone, attempting to scare the people out of hell. The goal is to use fear to save people. Of course, the opposite of that is to focus on people's desire for heaven. Given the choice between hell and heaven, most people choose heaven. Another fear often used in evangelism is a fear of Christ's second coming. Others proclaim false promises of health and wealth in order to gain a following. Finally, some only discuss Jesus' claims, debating whether he is a liar, a lunatic, or Lord. This tactic attempts to use reason to convince people of the Gospel. All of these methods have some success, as people respond to what they are told or how they feel emotionally.

However, did Jesus use these methods when he proclaimed the

Gospel of the Kingdom? He certainly talked about some of these issues, but he never made them his focus in evangelism. None of these were his *method* of evangelism.

The Bible in evangelism

Many methods of evangelism rely, at some point, on convincing people that the Bible is authoritative for what must be believed. Proponents of these methods teach we must first convince people of the truth or reliability of the Bible. However, Jesus never made that an issue.

Jesus dealt with people who accepted various portions of the Bible. Not only was there no New Testament, Jews differed on their acceptance and rejection of different books circulating in their day. Jesus used what people already accepted. When he talked with the Sadducees, he used the Law since they rejected the rest of the Old Testament. When he talked with the Pharisees, he also used the Psalms and Prophets since they regarded those as from God.

Although many accepted the Old Testament as authoritative, this was not a universal position. Jesus dealt with Gentiles and Samaritans who had other writings and beliefs they considered to be truthful. Jesus never made convincing people of the authority of religious writings his starting point. If people accepted the authority of the writings, he would refer to them. Nevertheless, he did not appear too concerned with convincing people which writings were acceptable and which were not.

Convincing people of the Bible was a non-issue for Jesus. The moment we make it one in evangelism, we are forced to defend that position before we can continue presenting the Gospel, regardless of whether we are talking to atheists, agnostics, Muslims, or Hindus. And even when dealing with someone who accepts the Bible as authoritative, we need to keep focused on the Gospel, lest the discussion digress to issues of interpretation or transmission of the documents.

Confronting ethical systems

Jesus focused people's attention on his Kingdom, always confronting them on one issue. His concern was the difference between a person's value system and God's value system. One of the clearest examples of Jesus' method is in his discussion with the rich, young man.[1]

1. See Chapter 14: The Value System of the Kingdom.

This is certainly not the only case of Jesus using this method, but it is one of the most significant.

When the young man approached Jesus, he asked which good deed he must do to have eternal life.[2] Since only God is good, Jesus told the man that in order to be good, he must be like God. The commandments were intended to reveal God's likeness to man. Keeping the commandments, however, is merely a first step in learning goodness. To truly become good, one's character must be like God's.

In answering the man's question, Jesus began listing several negative commandments—the "You shall not" commandments. These are the easiest for us to hear because we can check them off in our minds, "I didn't do that one, and I didn't do that one..." Then Jesus turned to the positive commandment to honor your father and mother. At this point, Jesus had listed representative commandments from the Decalogue,[3] the very laws this young man considered himself to have kept.

The last commandment Jesus gave the man was to love his neighbor as he loved himself. This is another way of saying the Golden Rule: Do unto others as you would have them do unto you. It is also another way of saying sacrificial love for the benefit of others. This is the fullness of God's value system. It is the cornerstone of everything Jesus taught. Jesus told the young man that in order to have eternal life he must adopt Jesus' value system.

Why did the man come to Jesus in the first place? Did he merely want Jesus to pat him on the back and tell him he was doing a good job? No, he came because he was empty inside. He had practiced the Law, but he was not changed by it. He did not know God because he had not been changed in his heart, and his value system had not been changed. The way we know God is by becoming like him. We become like him only by becoming sacrificial lovers.

The man only reflected the likeness of God to the extent he practiced the Law, but he was not like God in his heart. He partially reflected God's glory, but he was never transformed, becoming glorious himself. Rules can change behavior, but not the heart; and without heart change, there can be no true relationship with God.

Jesus gave this man instruction to help him see what was missing in his life and to help him find the path to eternal life. He told him that

2. Matthew 19:16-20:16

3. "The Decalogue" is another name for the Ten Commandments.

if he wanted to be perfect (perfect means to be like God) he must sell his possessions and give to the poor. The man *said* he loved his neighbor, but now Jesus was trying to help the man *truly* love his neighbor. Saying and doing are two different things. The man *believed* he loved his neighbor as himself, but he *did not* love his neighbor as himself.

If the young man would adopt the value system of God and begin doing to others as he wanted done to him, and if he truly loved his neighbor as himself, then he would be transformed on the inside. However, until the man admitted he loved himself and his wealth more than other people, he would not be able to change in his heart.

The only way he could follow Jesus was to be like Jesus. He would have to sell his possessions and give to the poor if he wanted to be in Jesus' Kingdom.[4] To enter Christ's Kingdom you must adopt his value system. To follow Jesus is to be like him, and to be like him is to be good. To be good is to be like God.

This rich man was seeking eternal life; but until he was ready to adopt Jesus' value system, he could not enter the Kingdom, which is the only place where eternal life is found. The young man went sorrowfully away from Jesus because he had great wealth accompanied by a great love for self. Did he enter Jesus' Kingdom? No, he did not. The Gospel of the Kingdom is a call to relinquish our values and replace them with God's.

Jesus evangelized by confronting people on their ethics. First, he taught them his value system of sacrificial love for the benefit of others. Then, he examined their values, asking them whether they saw the difference. That is how Jesus talked to people. Jesus required people to compare themselves to him based solely on the issue of sacrificial love.

Matters like heaven and hell were incidental to Jesus' message. His method of evangelism was inviting people to join his Kingdom with the clear understanding that they would have to change their value systems to enter it. If we wish to practice evangelism as Jesus did, we need to discuss the differences between the value system a person holds and the value system of Jesus. We must ask them whether or not their life is characterized and driven by sacrificial love for the benefit of others.

When we focus our message on the Gospel of the Kingdom (the

---

4. Jesus was not requiring the man to become destitute. This man was considered rich, possessing financial wealth far in excess of his personal need (see Appendix: Jesus' Finances).

King, his value system, and the requirement of adopting it), we no longer need to argue about the Bible, evolution, or other matters we may deem as important.[5] We only need to clearly understand the Gospel and discuss it with others as a value system and a Kingdom. This is the call Jesus gave, and it should be the call we use as well.

The advantage of this method is that we do not need to know every answer to every question of history, science, and religion; we only need to know the Gospel of the Kingdom. We only need to discuss Jesus' value system and compare it to the other person's. Jesus called people to his value system and spiritual Kingdom. He was not asking them to join an earthly kingdom or organization; he was asking people to change on the inside and become good by being like him.

Doing evangelism as Jesus did simplifies the issue. There is no need to convince people about the Bible or its source, transmission, inspiration, authenticity, lack of corruption, or anything else. No matter what a person's tradition or interpretation, both the basic ideas contained in the Bible and the tradition in all branches of Christianity agree on one thing: the Gospel of the Kingdom. That is, God's value system was demonstrated on the cross for us and we need to be transformed to loving others in that same way.

Neither do we need to know everything about a person's background or religion. We need only have them compare their god or ethical system with Jesus. Which one is better? Which one produces better relationships? Which one transforms lives? Which one can really change the world? There is only one God and only one way to have relationship with him.

Jesus did not hesitate to call the rich, young man to his value system, as difficult as that call was. He did not merely say, "Follow me." He defined what it meant to follow him.

Jesus' instruction was not intended only for this one man in this one specific circumstance. Seeking to escape the requirement Jesus places on all his disciples, many claim that what Jesus said to the rich man does not apply to them. We know the requirement is broader than this one man because Jesus said it was difficult for rich *people* to

5. This is not to say issues of biblical authority, science and philosophy are not important or have no bearing on issues of faith. However, the work of the Holy Spirit in convicting the world of sin, righteousness, and judgment only requires we demonstrate God's love and man's falling short of it (John 16:8-15).

enter the Kingdom.[6] Those who have wealth and love it more than Jesus must consider whether they are truly in his Kingdom, for they still waver over whose value system they follow. If you have a value system that places yourself first, you will have a difficult time entering Jesus' Kingdom. The more you possess, the more difficult it is to be a sacrificial lover.

The hindrance of religion

One night, a Pharisee named Nicodemus came to talk to Jesus.[7] In order to experience the transformation[8] he was seeking, Nicodemus needed to change his value system and thinking on several issues; so that is precisely what Jesus focused on with him.

The unique factor in Nicodemus' case was that he really believed he understood and knew God. Nicodemus' problem was his *religion*. The Pharisees could agree that others needed to repent of sin, but they did not see it as an issue for them. Nicodemus did not realize how far his value system was from God's, and how out of relationship with God he was because of that gap.

Nicodemus needed to truly see who the King was to understand the Kingdom of God. Jesus told him the required change was a radical new birth, because new birth was the only way he could enter this Kingdom.

> *Jesus answered, "Truly, truly, I say to you, unless one is born of water and the Spirit, he cannot enter the kingdom of God. That which is born of the flesh is flesh, and that which is born of the Spirit is spirit."*[9]

When Jesus said, "water and spirit," he was referring to John the Baptist's testimony of who Jesus was.[10] Nicodemus needed to be transformed to enter the Kingdom. He needed to accept the testimony of John the Baptist about the King and the Kingdom, and he needed to be born again. He could not keep his old ideas intact; he required a brand new start.

---

6. Matthew 19:23
7. John 3
8. The book of John is all about transformation.
9. John 3:5-6
10. John 1:33 I myself did not know him, but he who sent me to baptize with water said to me, 'He on whom you see the Spirit descend and remain, this is he who baptizes with the Holy Spirit.'

Jesus then challenged Nicodemus' interpretation of Scripture. Nicodemus would have to give up the belief that he was right about his religion. What Nicodemus valued most was, unfortunately, a wrong view of God.[11] He liked to think he understood the Scriptures, but he really did not. In order to know God, he would have to trust that Jesus was right about the issue of value system.

The final problem for Nicodemus was his understanding of sin. When Nicodemus taught the story of Moses lifting the bronze serpent up on the pole,[12] he considered himself to be like Moses; but he needed to see himself as a rebellious Israelite.[13] Once Jesus died on the cross, Nicodemus believed what Jesus said about the Kingdom and his need for a Savior.[14]

As a Pharisee, the values Nicodemus believed to be God's values were not God's at all. In order to be saved, he had to acknowledge his value system was far from God's. He had to abandon approaching God by works and recognize his relationship with God could not be restored until he was willing to start all over again in Christ's Kingdom with the value system of the King.

Relational failure

On another occasion, Jesus deliberately journeyed through Samaria to meet a Samaritan woman who came to draw water from a well.[15] Jesus told her he could supply what she was truly thirsting for: living water. However, before she could receive this from him, she had to admit her thirst. His living water is only for those who will change their value systems. It is not for those who want to continue in a life of sin.

The woman was a social outcast at the other end of the spectrum from Nicodemus, being his opposite in every way. Nevertheless, she

---

11. John 3:9-12 Nicodemus said to him, "How can these things be?" Jesus answered him, "Are you the teacher of Israel and yet you do not understand these things? Truly, truly, I say to you, we speak of what we know, and bear witness to what we have seen, but you do not receive our testimony. If I have told you earthly things and you do not believe, how can you believe if I tell you heavenly things?"

12. Numbers 21

13. John 3:14-15 And as Moses lifted up the serpent in the wilderness, so must the Son of Man be lifted up, that whoever believes in him may have eternal life.

14. Nicodemus gave Jesus a royal burial in terms of the amount of spices used (John 19:39).

15. John 4

needed transformation as much as he did. To reveal the place of her thirst, Jesus discussed her relationships. She had been married five times and was currently living with another man whom she had not married. Obviously, this woman had great desires and great failures in terms of relationship.

Jesus also discussed with her what God deems as true worship. She was preoccupied with the place and *method* of worshiping God, but Jesus wanted her to see that God required *relationship* with him in spirit and truth. She needed to be transformed in her value system if she was going to find living water.

The woman at the well was thirsty for relational transformation, and she was invited by Christ to come and find satisfaction.[16] Her relationships in this life could only be transformed once her relationship with God was transformed. Worship of God is a transformation of value system.

God requires we abandon our wicked thoughts and ways and replace them with his ways and his thoughts.[17] In order to have his living water—the power of relationship—springing up inside of us, we must first take his value system into our hearts.

The unchanged man

There is an amazing story in which Jesus healed a man who had been lame for thirty-eight years.[18] One remarkable feature of this event is that the man had not come to Jesus for healing. In fact, the man had no faith in Jesus at all; he did not even know who Jesus was.

Jesus told the man, "Take up your mat and walk." After being healed, the man was confronted by the Pharisees for carrying his mat

---

16. Beginning with the transformation of water into wine, Isaiah 55 becomes thematic in John. It speaks of the need to enter into an everlasting covenant with God by adopting his value system and relinquishing one's own.

Isaiah 55:1 Come, everyone who thirsts, come to the waters; and he who has no money, come, buy and eat! Come, buy wine and milk without money and without price.

17. Isaiah 55:6-9 Seek the Lord while he may be found; call upon him while he is near; let the wicked forsake his way, and the unrighteous man his thoughts; let him return to the Lord, that he may have compassion on him, and to our God, for he will abundantly pardon. For my thoughts are not your thoughts, neither are your ways my ways, declares the Lord. For as the heavens are higher than the earth, so are my ways higher than your ways and my thoughts than your thoughts.

18. John 5

since this was the Sabbath and they did not consider mat-carrying to be a lawful activity. When they asked him who told him to carry his mat, the man was unable to identify Jesus since he did not know who had healed him.

Later, Jesus found the man at the temple and gave him an unusual warning. "See, you are well! Sin no more, that nothing worse may happen to you." As terrible as physical suffering can be, it is not as bad as being out of relationship with God. The man had been externally transformed, yet he had not been internally transformed. He was well in his body, but he was not well in his soul.

The man demonstrated his unchanged heart by immediately reporting Jesus to the Pharisees once he knew his identity. Although obvious to him that the Jews were not pleased with his healer, he refused to heed Jesus' words about value system. He remained unchanged and out of relationship with Christ, choosing to betray Jesus rather than follow him.

Proclaim the true Gospel

We need to follow Jesus' method of evangelism. When Jesus called people to enter his Kingdom, it always included leaving their own kingdoms. In our own kingdoms, we choose what we value: wealth, security, pleasure, religious ideas and theology, and relational methods unlike Christ's. The list of values that can keep us from following Jesus is very long, and the only way to follow Christ is to give them all up.

Entering Christ's Kingdom requires that we adopt his value system of sacrificial love. It is a call to change how we treat others and how we respond in relationship. We must humbly put aside our ideas of what it means to please God, and accept only what the King declares as acceptable. Any proclamation of the Kingdom that neglects value system is not good news, and it is not the Gospel.

31 Our Motive for Following Christ

It is important to understand the various motivations people have for coming to Christ. By distinguishing between the right and wrong reasons people want to know about Jesus, we can focus our attention on presenting the Gospel clearly and without giving people a false impression of what Christianity is truly about.

Some come to Jesus for wealth; their motivation is financial. Having been told the lie that Jesus will make them rich, some come out of greed, while others seek to solve financial problems. Jesus made it clear that trying to serve both wealth and him was like having two different masters, making deep allegiance to him impossible.[1]

The prime example of this is Judas.[2] His motivation for following Jesus was financial gain. He believed there would be an earthly kingdom and that he would gain great wealth through it. People who teach that God will make you rich are more like Judas than Jesus. Do not be surprised when they betray you. In the end, when dreams of wealth do not work out as desired, these followers often sell Jesus out.

Another reason people come to Jesus is for hope of health or healing. Many stories in the New Testament contain this element, as it

---

1. Matthew 6:24 No one can serve two masters, for either he will hate the one and love the other, or he will be devoted to the one and despise the other. You cannot serve God and money.

2. Matthew 26:14-15 Then one of the twelve, whose name was Judas Iscariot, went to the chief priests and said, "What will you give me if I deliver him over to you?" And they paid him thirty pieces of silver.

was very normal for people to come to him when he was healing so liberally. The problem for many of these people was that they sought healing rather than the King. This was why Jesus pointed out the great faith of those who recognized his authority.[3] Today, those who come to Jesus seeking healing often leave disillusioned because they do not receive what people have falsely promised on God's behalf. They do not realize their greater need is a change inside their hearts.

Others claim to follow Christ only because someone offers them a free lunch. Jesus rebuked a whole crowd of people who wished to make him king only because he fed them.[4] Homeless people, or people in areas of famine, will often listen to Christians as long as food is offered. Some people in prison take advantage of the generosity of Christians without any intent of changing their lives. When the bread stops coming easily, these people quickly move on.

Some people follow Jesus for the sake of their children. Unlike those who brought their children to Christ to have him bless them,[5] these people may have been away from church for years. Now that they have children they feel a need to expose them to God. This is not a bad thing, for one should seek God's blessing for one's family. However, people like this often turn away from Christ when their children do not appear to be getting better, when their children grow up and leave home, or when the children themselves show signs of disinterest in God. Since they try to instill a faith in their children that they themselves do not possess, they should not be surprised when this effort fails.

There are also those who come to see miracles. Some seek the supernatural, looking for a sign or proof that God is real. Although their motive is a bit different than the Pharisees to whom Jesus spoke,[6]

---

3. See Chapter 9: The Authority of the King

4. John 6:26 Jesus answered them, "Truly, truly, I say to you, you are seeking me, not because you saw signs, but because you ate your fill of the loaves."

5. Matthew 19:13-15 Then children were brought to him that he might lay his hands on them and pray. The disciples rebuked the people, but Jesus said, "Let the little children come to me and do not hinder them, for to such belongs the kingdom of heaven." And he laid his hands on them and went away.

6. Matthew 12:38-40 Then some of the scribes and Pharisees answered him, saying, "Teacher, we wish to see a sign from you." But he answered them, "An evil and adulterous generation seeks for a sign, but no sign will be given to it except the sign of the prophet Jonah. For just as Jonah was three days and three nights in the belly of the great fish, so will the Son of Man be three days and three nights in the heart of the earth."

the basic principle of needing proof before faith is the same. If you do not have faith that God raises the dead, then you will never believe. Miracles will never be enough to convince you of what you cannot see.

Another group of people follow Jesus because they are seeking someone to overthrow their oppressors. Their goals are much like the insurrectionist Jews who wanted to overthrow the Romans, and like those who hated paying taxes to Caesar.[7] Overthrowing an evil oppressor may be a good cause, but one must not claim to do it in the name of the Messiah. Jesus did not come to establish an earthly kingdom as many Jews desired. Christians must not fall into this same error. Some follow Jesus assuming he will be on their side when they fight a battle, but Jesus never intended for us to kill or rebel in his name.

Other people come to Jesus for power. Some seek power over sin in their lives, that they might be free from a life-dominating sin. This is good, but many become discouraged when they have trouble defeating sin, or when they realize this one particular sin is simply the tip of the iceberg. True Christians learn they are a lot more sinful than they first realized. The power Jesus promises is real, but not magical. His power works along with our desire to adopt his value system. Unless we seek to change in the manner by which the Holy Spirit operates, we will be disappointed with the results.

Some follow Jesus in order to have power over others. Many of Jesus' disciples argued among themselves over who would or should have the most authority.[8] Only the naïve think that churches are exempt from people with this attitude. Some love to have power and use Christianity as a means to it. History is filled with examples of such people. They use religion to gain power over others in order to use them and exploit them.

Others come to Jesus simply to avoid judgment. They have heard of God's judgment and are terrified of the thought of hell. Whole revivals have been based on this idea alone. Unfortunately, the love of sin in this life may be more powerful for them than the fear of what might come after death; so many are deceived into thinking they are going to heaven even though they have never entered the Kingdom of God.

---

7. Matthew 22:17

8. Matthew 20:20-21 Then the mother of the sons of Zebedee came up to him with her sons, and kneeling before him she asked him for something. And he said to her, "What do you want?" She said to him, "Say that these two sons of mine are to sit, one at your right hand and one at your left, in your kingdom."

Those are several of the selfish reasons for which people come to Jesus. The problem with any selfish reason for following Christ is that it is the wrong reason and the wrong motivation. If a person comes for the wrong reason, he is likely to leave for the wrong reason as well. Unless a person is transformed from idolatry to reality, he will always be one disappointment away from rejecting Christ.

Fear and difficulty often lead a person to Christ, and that is not a problem. The problem is evangelism that focuses on false promises. Unless the reason a person comes to Christ changes to a true understanding of the Gospel, the person lives in idolatry and may not really be part of the Kingdom.

Follow Christ for what you cannot lose

How does someone gain eternal life? He must believe the true Gospel of the Kingdom, and he must believe correctly about Christ's sacrificial death. However, that is not enough; he must also be transformed into a sacrificial lover.

When Christ called people to follow him, he always made sure they understood what he expected of them. He was ready to turn people away if they were not willing to adopt his value system. Life in his Kingdom is not about selfish gain, but about sacrificial service. Jesus told his disciples, "If anyone would come after me, let him deny himself and take up his cross and follow me."[9]

Remember, the greatest picture of the love of God is Christ on the cross. To be like him, you must be a sacrificial lover. Jesus wants us to be like him with a willingness to suffer for others. Taking up the cross is not only about a willingness to die for Jesus. It is a willingness to die for others, and for their benefit.

When the mother of James and John came to Jesus requesting a special position in Christ's Kingdom for her sons, here is what transpired:

> *Jesus answered, "You do not know what you are asking. Are you able to drink the cup that I am to drink?" They said to him, "We are able." He said to them, "You will drink my cup, but to sit at my right hand and at my left is not mine to grant, but it is for those for whom it has been prepared by my Father." And when the ten heard it, they were indignant at the two brothers.*

9. Matthew 16:24

> *But Jesus called them to him and said, "You know that the rulers of the Gentiles lord it over them, and their great ones exercise authority over them. It shall not be so among you. But whoever would be great among you must be your servant, and whoever would be first among you must be your slave, even as the Son of Man came not to be served but to serve, and to give his life as a ransom for many."*[10]

Following Jesus involves drinking the cup as he did. His cup is sacrificial love for the benefit of others—his cup is his death on the cross. Christ-likeness is about becoming like Christ. If that is your motivation for following Christ, then no one can ever take that away from you.

Paul asked, and then answered, this question: "What can separate us from the love of Christ?"[11] He said that tribulation, distress, persecution, famine, nakedness, danger, and death could not do it. He said that we would conquer and be conformed to the image of Christ in spite of those hardships.[12] The reason these difficulties cannot separate us from God is that they are not the reasons we follow Christ. Since we do not follow him to avoid tribulation, distress, persecution, famine, or death; then the loss of our wealth, health, or life will never stop us from following him.

When we love as Jesus loves, we know that we know him because we are like him. We know that we are in his love because his love flows through us. When we follow Jesus for the right reason—the reason *he gave* in calling us—we will never be disappointed with him, nor will we ever turn away from him.

---

10. Matthew 20:22-28

11. Romans 8:35, 37-39 Who shall separate us from the love of Christ? Shall tribulation, or distress, or persecution, or famine, or nakedness, or danger, or sword? ... No, in all these things we are more than conquerors through him who loved us. For I am sure that neither death nor life, nor angels nor rulers, nor things present nor things to come, nor powers, nor height nor depth, nor anything else in all creation, will be able to separate us from the love of God in Christ Jesus our Lord.

12. Romans 8:28-29 And we know that for those who love God all things work together for good, for those who are called according to his purpose. For those whom he foreknew he also predestined to be conformed to the image of his Son, in order that he might be the firstborn among many brothers.

32 Correct Biblical Interpretation

The foundation for everything in the Gospel is quite simple. There is a part that we believe and a part that we do, and ultimately what we are called to believe is tied to what we are called to do. We believe in God's sacrificial love for our benefit, and we adopt his loving treatment of others as our own value system. This simple understanding ought to be the basis for all study and interpretation of the New Testament.

When we approach any text in the New Testament, we must begin by asking what it has to do with the Gospel of the Kingdom: What does this passage of Scripture teach us about God's sacrificial love for us, and how does it teach us to have sacrificial love for others? This simple approach helps us distinguish between the Gospel and any application of the Gospel.

The Gospel is what is required for salvation, the bare minimum it takes to be called a Christian. As outlined earlier,[1] there are only a few key doctrines that a person must believe in order to be saved. That belief must also be accompanied by the evidence of salvation: the adoption of God's value system. Knowing this helps us understand that the majority of the New Testament is an elaboration on the Gospel. It is illustrative material to help believers live the value system of God by knowing what it looks like in practice.

By making this distinction, we are preserved from making laws out of Gospel application, and then erroneously using those laws to

1. See Part 3: The Gospel of the Kingdom

create for ourselves new gospels that are not gospels at all. Adding certain behavioral requirements to the Gospel that are not part of the Gospel itself has been an error since Paul's day. Even he had to confront Jews who habitually sought to force his Gentile converts to adopt Jewish practices.

When approaching a New Testament text, you should seek to discover what it teaches about sacrificial love. As you identify items in terms of God's value system, you will become wise in distinguishing principle, application, and interpretation from the Gospel itself. You will learn to see that each passage is intended to teach you how you might become more like God. The transformation comes through a growing understanding of value system, and not through rules or legal requirements of law.

For example, if you examine Romans 12, you will find the opening verses describe the believer's obligation in the Gospel to have sacrificial love as his worship of God.[2] Then, the rest of that chapter, as well as the following chapters, illustrate and amplify the practice of that kind of love. The illustrations help us gain understanding into God's love and his value system. However, you would be mistaken to begin taking them as rules to follow rather than as teaching to further your understanding of God's love.

The Gospel is about love, not law

To understand the message of the New Testament, you must understand the intent of its authors. If you are confused about what they were trying to communicate, you will fail to come away with a correct understanding of how you are to live. Once you begin thinking in terms of God's value system and see it as the theme of the New Testament, it will make understanding and applying the Bible much easier.

Matthew sought to show us the true Kingdom of God and how we may be part of it by adopting the King's value system. Peter told us how to live as God's people in this world. James wanted us to live the faith we claim to possess. John wanted us to believe his witness of Christ in order that we might be transformed. Paul wanted to make sure we experience the glorification that accompanies our faith in Christ.[3] That transformation comes by the Spirit, and not by the Law.[4]

2. See Chapter 26: Worship and Holiness
3. See Appendix: Justification, Sanctification, and Glorification
4. Galatians 3

None of the authors intended to give us a list of rules to follow. The New Testament is not a new set of laws to which we must conform. It does not teach this, and the authors did not intend this as they were writing. What they did write was instruction on the Gospel message and how to be part of the Kingdom of God. They gave examples of what participation in the Kingdom looked like in the lives and relationships of all those who were in the Kingdom. They taught transformation through becoming like Christ.

When the first council of the Church gathered in Jerusalem to discuss the place of Gentiles alongside Jews within the Church, they concluded that Gentiles should abstain from that which offended Jews.[5] They recognized the Gentiles as equal brothers and sisters in Christ, but they did not want brother destroying brother over differences in interpretation, heritage, or conscience. They were discussing the *application* of the Gospel in light of different traditions. They agreed on the Gospel and gave practical application of what love for one another required. (They also addressed the issue of sexual immorality, which is an issue of love. Sexual immorality is not love, an error common today and throughout human history.)

The Kingdom of God is about following Christ in his Kingdom. It is a release from the Law. Being part of Christ's Kingdom is not a matter of following rules, but of becoming a lover as he is. Love fulfills the Law.[6] That is why we do not need the Law anymore.

The whole point of Galatians is the believer's freedom from legalistic bondage.[7] Paul did not teach Gentiles to follow the Law since it was no longer necessary. What is necessary is a transformation of the heart. Once you are guided by sacrificial love, you no longer focus on lists of rules or laws.[8] You use your mind to contemplate how sacri-

---

5. Acts 15

6. Romans 13:8-10 Owe no one anything, except to love each other, for the one who loves another has fulfilled the law. The commandments, "You shall not commit adultery, You shall not murder, You shall not steal, You shall not covet," and any other commandment, are summed up in this word: "You shall love your neighbor as yourself." Love does no wrong to a neighbor; therefore love is the fulfilling of the law.

7. Galatians 5:13-14 For you were called to freedom, brothers. Only do not use your freedom as an opportunity for the flesh, but through love serve one another. For the whole law is fulfilled in one word: "You shall love your neighbor as yourself."

8. Matthew 7:12 So whatever you wish that others would do to you, do also to them, for this is the Law and the Prophets.

Matthew 22:37-40 And he said to him, "You shall love the Lord your God with all

ficial love should behave in each situation and relationship in which you find yourself. Using the Gospel as the foundation, the principle of sacrificial love becomes the guide for how believers should live in various times, cultures, and circumstances.

The authors of the New Testament sought to help us clearly see what Christ-like love was like: how it acted, lived, and sacrificed. Living in relationship requires sacrificial love, and not burdensome obligations. Otherwise, division will persist regarding the rules because we will constantly disagree on how to interpret them. We will differ on the who, how, when, and why of the rules. Rather than see us unified because of our mutual faith in the Gospel, the world will see us divided.

Loving God and others out of obligation, rules, or law is like a husband and wife that do what is right for one another because they must, and not because they love each other. They are obedient in what they do for each other, but the action flows from obligation, and not from the heart. God does not want us to love others because we *must*, but because it flows naturally from our changed hearts.

Knowledge does not make you spiritual. Love for God and others is the true measure of spirituality. Knowledge guides love, but never overrules it. *All* our actions should be done in love, whether instructing or serving. If we believe we are to do something and we do it even when it is unloving, we have become like the Corinthians.[9]

Some Christians are so concerned with promoting their idea of what is right that they will do it in an unloving way. If we practice what we believe to be true without regard for the effect it has on others, we do not really know what we think we know. Reducing Christianity to rules and laws is to be like the pharisaism Christ condemned.[10]

Many Christians have lost their way by seeking rules and laws to

---

your heart and with all your soul and with all your mind. This is the great and first commandment. And a second is like it: You shall love your neighbor as yourself. On these two commandments depend all the Law and the Prophets."

9. 1 Corinthians 8:1-3 This "knowledge" puffs up, but love builds up. If anyone imagines that he knows something, he does not yet know as he ought to know. But if anyone loves God, he is known by God.

10. Matthew 23:23-24 Woe to you, scribes and Pharisees, hypocrites! For you tithe mint and dill and cumin, and have neglected the weightier matters of the law: justice and mercy and faithfulness. These you ought to have done, without neglecting the others. You blind guides, straining out a gnat and swallowing a camel!

follow. Some seek to make Old Testament laws the laws of the land. Others take bizarre interpretations from partial texts, or allege nitpicky interpretations based on obscure words. They create rules for Christians based on a faulty understanding of the Gospel and a strained interpretation of the Bible.

When we lose focus on what the Gospel of the Kingdom is, and how it should change how we relate to one another, we travel a path guaranteed to bring heartache and relational destruction. We must understand the Gospel correctly and use it as our sole basis for understanding the Bible.

Actions are only right if they flow from a right heart

The Bible teaches us Christ-likeness, which is true Christian ethics. It teaches us sacrificial love. But if we search the Bible for rules to be discovered and followed, the Gospel loses its transforming power.

An example of how this happens is the issue of giving financially to God's work and those in need. Since Gentile Christians were never under the Law, they were never required to give a tithe or any percent of their income to God. In the Church, giving is not prescribed.[11] Rather, it is a freedom we have that flows from transformed hearts yearning to lovingly sacrifice for others.

According to God, it is more important to have the right motivation before doing the right thing. It is more important to have a sacrificial heart first, and then to give, rather than give out of obligation. Doing the right action without the right heart is worthless in the sight of God. Although you might do the right thing, you are not doing it because you are like him. After you adopt the value system of the King, giving that pleases God will naturally flow from you. Otherwise, you are only reflecting the likeness of God without actually becoming like him.

Even today, pastors and churches call on their congregations to give ten percent, the tithe of the Jews under the Old Covenant. Although this is not even New Testament instruction, people are pressured into giving reluctantly. Those spiritual leaders should be ashamed of themselves for teaching something God does not demand or require. They should be ashamed that they cause people to give in a way that dishon-

---

11. 2 Corinthians 9:7 Each one must give as he has made up his mind, not reluctantly or under compulsion, for God loves a cheerful giver.

ors God.[12]

We are to give to extend the Kingdom, yet not in quantitative terms or by percent. God requires we live and give *sacrificially*. He desires our hearts to first be transformed so that when we give it is real and not compulsory. He wants us to become givers like *he* is.

Examine what you believe in light of your calling to be Christ-like. Be careful about interpretations that are more pharisaical than Christian. Make sure you understand the New Covenant. Christ's death was to save you and to make you like him. It was not to replace old laws with new ones, but to abolish dependence on law that we might learn love. His death was for our glorious transformation into his likeness by the power of the Holy Spirit.

12. Worse than this is coercion to give even beyond an individual's means. Jesus called it the "devouring widow's houses" and connected it to the judgment against the temple and its rulers (Mark 12:38-13:2; Luke 20:45-21:6). Those with power and wealth pressured the poor to give rather than sought to meet their needs. The widow's offering is not exemplary sacrificial giving; Jesus was pointing out how she was being exploited. The religious leaders sought to please their appetites, gain prestige, and have power and wealth at the expense of even the destitute.

33 Communion

Christian churches continue to break bread and drink the fruit of the vine as a regular tradition, yet it did not take long before many in the early Church developed mystical ideas about the bread and wine. John's account of the last supper Jesus ate with his disciples is interesting because he left out the sharing of bread and wine. Instead of this, John related a story in which Jesus washed the feet of his disciples.[1] John wanted to make sure the *importance* of the meal was not lost in the *ritual* of the meal.

During the supper, not prior to it, Jesus showed his love for his disciples by washing their feet. It was an act so deliberate as to never be forgotten. Jesus' loving service came from a deep self-knowledge of what would happen at the cross. There he would fulfill his Father's mission, and once again return to his Father.[2]

The most important part of the lesson Jesus taught is often missed by focusing on the act of footwashing. By washing his disciples' feet, Jesus intended his disciples to learn what "clean" really meant. When Jesus approached Peter to wash his feet, Peter flatly refused him.[3] Pe-

1. John 13:1-21

2. John 13:3-4 Jesus, knowing that the Father had given all things into his hands, and that he had come from God and was going back to God, rose from supper. He laid aside his outer garments, and taking a towel, tied it around his waist.

3. John 13:6-8 He came to Simon Peter, who said to him, "Lord, do you wash my feet?" Jesus answered him, "What I am doing you do not understand now, but afterward you will understand." Peter said to him, "You shall never wash my feet."

ter believed Jesus' actions placed Jesus beneath Peter, since he did not understand that what Jesus was doing was actually symbolic of what he would do at the cross. Peter was foolishly refusing to be taught by the Master. By disagreeing and arguing, he was raising himself to the level of teacher.

Jesus told Peter, "If I do not wash you, you have no share with me." Peter took Jesus' response to mean he could not continue fellowshipping with Jesus at the table unless Jesus washed him. So Peter then wanted to be completely washed. Yet again, Jesus had to tell Peter he had it wrong. The one who has bathed is clean and does not require another bath; he only needs to clean his feet.

The point is simple: unless Christ serves you at the cross, you cannot have fellowship with him. We cannot come to Christ unless we allow him to serve us, washing us at the cross. Without the cross, which is the place that most fully demonstrates God's serving love, we cannot be made clean.

Cleanness for the Christian comes through repentance. Repentance is turning from choosing your own value system to adopting God's. This happens when we come to Christ. It is what happens when a heart is prepared to come to the King. Jesus was tying the idea of footwashing to being forgiven at the cross.

Repentance is a lifelong experience for the believer. Like Peter, who did not humbly accept what Christ was doing when he came to wash his feet, we must repent whenever we recognize we are promoting our own will rather than Christ's. By first refusing Jesus, Peter sought to impose his value system on him; but it was Peter, not Christ, who needed to change.

Another proof that footwashing is about the cross is how Jesus spoke about Judas. Jesus said that all of his disciples were clean except Judas.[4] Judas was not clean because he never repented; he never adopted the value system of the King or the Kingdom. He never received the forgiveness of the cross.

It is striking to think that, even at this point, the disciples had no idea what would happen at the cross. They still had no idea the true purpose of the Messiah was to remove sin and make people spiritually clean. They were still anticipating another kind of kingdom. They

4. John 13:11 For he knew who was to betray him; that was why he said, "Not all of you are clean."

were still struggling with issues of greatness and superiority.

The disciples had not offered to wash each other's feet that night because their understanding of God's sacrificial love for them was still incomplete. You must accept God's sacrificial love for you before you can truly become a sacrificial lover like God. You must acknowledge and accept his value system before you can fully adopt it as your own, because *that* kind of love must first be experienced prior to emulating it. A true knowledge of the King and the value system of the Kingdom, especially forgiveness, is crucial to transformation.

Jesus calls us to follow his example, but not by washing feet. The example he intends his disciples to follow is one of servanthood. He wants our lives to be characterized by humble, sacrificial service. Unless you practice sacrificial love, you still think you are greater than the Master. You might think, "No, I am not as great as Jesus." However, *in reality* your lack of service betrays how you consider yourself too exceptional to serve others. You think you are exceptional because, for some reason, you are making exceptions as to why you do not need to serve. But, as a Christian, no act of service is beneath you.

Note that Jesus never asked the disciples to wash his feet, but to wash one another's feet. This is a much more difficult task. Since Christ makes footwashing akin to forgiveness here, what he is really asking us to do is to be mindful of our need to forgive.

Footwashing is about cleaning. It is about helping one another deal with the sin in our lives. You wash my feet when you lovingly stoop to help remove the dirt of sin from my life. When someone comes to help clean your feet, you must acknowledge your feet are dirty.

We *all* have dirty feet in some way. We must never reject the one who comes to help make them clean. Doing so is really a rejection of the one the washer is following, obeying, and emulating. It is Jesus who makes us clean by the cross, but we all need others to humbly, lovingly, and gently come and wash our feet when we have something in our lives that needs to change.

Various Christian traditions have followed, as a rule, the command to wash feet. However, unless they understand the true meaning of Christ's command, they do not improve relationships. Knowing that the footwashing Jesus had in mind here is forgiveness among his disciples helps us understand how we are to act toward one another in relationship.

Walking away from a relationship with another Christian because he has "dirty feet" that you have not offered to wash demonstrates an attitude completely unlike Christ's. Christ conquers sin in our lives *by* washing us, not by giving up on us. Therefore, we, too, must humbly offer to wash and forgive others.

When someone is unwilling to be washed, he is either like Peter or Judas. If he is like Judas, he rejects washing because he refuses to adopt Christ's value system into his life. If he is like Peter, he thinks he knows more than Jesus, the Master, does. Either way, if he continues in the unwashed state, he will find, as Jesus said, he can have no fellowship with him.

The Nature of Communion

As in all theology, the nature of Communion is relational. God intends for it to be a time of reflecting on his relationship with us, and also on our relationships with one another. The most significant thing we can do for one another is to forgive each other. When we do that, we are most like Christ.

Even as the Gospel has two parts, so does Communion. In the Gospel, we experience God's sacrificial love for us on the cross. He has reconciled us to himself and taken away our sin. This is the cup of Communion. Our fellowship with God depends solely on his work at the cross. His sacrificial love for us enables us to have relationship with him.

The second part of the Gospel is our sacrificial love for one another. We who are in the Kingdom practice the love demonstrated for us at the cross. Participation in the bread of Communion is our promise to one another that we will practice God's value system with each other. Communion is all about how we are to treat one another.[5] We are to treat each other the way God has treated us.

If you will not forgive and be at peace with those in the Church, *do not take the bread*, for that is what the bread signifies. If you do not want unity with Christ, and if you do not want to adopt his value system and have relationship with him, *do not take the cup*, for that is the meaning of the cup.

There is nothing magical about the cup and bread. They are only the symbols of a covenant: the New Covenant in God's blood. They are

5. 1 Corinthians 11:29 For anyone who eats and drinks without discerning the body eats and drinks judgment on himself.

the symbols we take to show we are in the promise of sacrificial love with one another.

I seek to teach my children what it means to "outdo one another in showing honor."[6] Since this is a difficult concept to understand, the day after my birthday I told them that the way they treated me on my birthday was the way they were supposed to treat each other every day. On a person's birthday, you want him to be first, to win, and to get special attention. You are less easily offended with him, and often more forgiving toward him.

We are to treat others like it is their birthday *every* day. That is what it means to take Communion. If you have never experienced the cup, you cannot experience the bread. No one can fully participate in the relationships of the Church who has not first experienced true relationship with God.

The cup represents our being washed by Christ. The bread is our promise to wash others like Christ washed us. To take the cup and bread, and yet be unforgiving and unloving, is the biggest lie you will ever practice.

Christian unity must flow from the Gospel

You become a Christian by believing the Gospel. This belief is demonstrated through accepting the crucial ideas taught by Christ and elaborated on by Paul, and through being willing to change because of that belief. Being a Christian involves your transformation to Christ-likeness through adopting God's value system. In other words, the Gospel has two parts: the part that you acknowledge as true and the resultant adoption of God's value system as your own.

Anything you believe beyond the Gospel is a matter of your traditions or interpretations of the teachings in the Bible. To say it another way, there is the one true Gospel and everything else beyond that is tradition and interpretation. The Gospel is the basis for our relationship with God, and God intends the Gospel alone to be the basis of our relationships with one another. That is why we must be careful not to add anything to the Gospel that damages relationships.

Paul taught that we are to accept all other believers as Christ has accepted us.[7] Since we are to accept all other believers of the Gospel,

6. Romans 12:10

7. Romans 15:7 Therefore welcome one another as Christ has welcomed you, for the glory of God.

regardless of their traditions and interpretations, we must make sure we really know exactly what the Gospel is and is not. Care must be taken to ensure that what we believe to be the Gospel truly is the Gospel—no more and no less.

Getting the Gospel right and getting God's value system right are inseparable. To know one is to know the other. The cross is the most perfect example of God's value system. It is the fullest expression of his love for others. It contains everything we need to know about God for salvation. The cross contains the essential points we need to believe, and it demonstrates how we are to live.

Christ's sacrifice is the basis of our own sacrificial living. Christlikeness is entirely about becoming like Christ. Becoming like him is adopting his value system and coming into his Kingdom.

We must live lives of reconciliation by remaining reconciled to God and by reconciling others to God. As we continue to understand God's value system more clearly, we recognize when we fail to live it. Whenever we replace love for self with love for others, we move into closer relationship with God. Our relationship with God is based solely on how much we share his value system. In fact, the *only* true measure of your spiritual life and health is how much your value system is like God's.

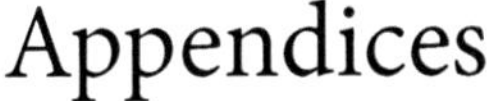

A The Significance of John the Baptist

In order to appreciate my interpretation of the Kingdom and prayer, it is important to bring together the many references to John the Baptist into one single, continuous picture. Although this repeats content previously discussed, it demonstrates more clearly how the work of John the Baptist has become our work in Christ's Kingdom.

John the Baptist is a very significant person in the Bible, especially in the book of Matthew. John came as the forerunner to Jesus, and he was the final Old Covenant prophet. God had not sent a prophet to the Jews for a very long time, so everyone was talking about him. He was an exciting figure and people wanted to know both who he was and what message he brought. John's message was simple: "The Kingdom of Heaven is at hand."[1]

John's message

John came to prepare the way for the King, Jesus, and to prepare for the coming of Jesus' Kingdom. John came in fulfillment of Isaiah's prophecy of the voice preparing the way for the coming King.[2]

> *A voice cries: "In the wilderness prepare the way of the Lord; make straight in the desert a highway for our God. Every valley*

1. Matthew 3:2

2. Matthew 3:3 For this is he who was spoken of by the prophet Isaiah when he said, "The voice of one crying in the wilderness: Prepare the way of the Lord; make his paths straight."

> *shall be lifted up, and every mountain and hill be made low; the uneven ground shall become level, and the rough places a plain. And the glory of the Lord shall be revealed, and all flesh shall see it together, for the mouth of the Lord has spoken."*[3]

When a king was coming to a town or city, the people would clear the road by which he was entering. They would remove debris and fill in the holes. They would make the way level and clear the path for his feet. That was the preparation for the coming of a king. When John the Baptist came, this was his work. He came to remove the bumps and fill in the potholes.

However, John the Baptist did not have a shovel. This might seem obvious to you or a silly way of saying it, but it is extremely important. If John had a shovel, he would have come to repair roads and his message would have been about enlisting more road repairmen. The purpose of fixing the roads would have been to prepare the path for the Messiah to enter Jerusalem. But he did not have a shovel.

We know the Kingdom of Heaven, the Kingdom of God,[4] is not an earthly kingdom because, if it were, John the Baptist would have had a shovel. If John came to fulfill Isaiah's prophecy as a literal preparer of roads, we would expect Jesus' Kingdom to be an earthly kingdom. Obviously, the place of preparation is not physical roads but within the hearts of men and women. The preparation is not external, but internal.

John came boldly proclaiming, "Repent!" Repentance is the relational issue of filling in the holes of the heart. It is removing the obstacles within you in preparation for the coming of Christ. The ministry of John the Baptist was to prepare the heart for a value system change. People can only receive the King once their hearts are prepared. In order to have Jesus as King in the heart, the mountains must be removed and the uneven ground must be made level.

Another aspect of John's ministry was warning people that judg-

---

3. Isaiah 40:3-5

4. There is no distinction between Kingdom of Heaven and Kingdom of God, as is made clear by Matthew 19:23-24.

Matthew 19:23-24 And Jesus said to his disciples, "Truly, I say to you, only with difficulty will a rich person enter the *kingdom of heaven*. Again I tell you, it is easier for a camel to go through the eye of a needle than for a rich person to enter the *kingdom of God*." (emphasis added)

ment was coming.[5] The King would judge and burn the chaff with unquenchable fire. This judgment was very important in the mind of John the Baptist.

John also came to reveal the identity of the Messiah to Israel.[6] Jesus came as the Spirit-anointed Son of David, while John came to ready a people for the King. John said that he baptized with water, but the Christ would baptize with the Holy Spirit.

Jesus told Nicodemus, "Unless one is born of water and the Spirit, he cannot enter the kingdom of God."[7] No one enters the Kingdom of God without first experiencing a heart preparation for the King. That was the purpose of John's baptism, whether done by John or by Jesus' disciples.[8] Once the heart becomes receptive to the King, Spirit baptism can take place.

John did not cease baptizing people once he revealed Jesus as Messiah. His work of preparing and pointing people to the King was not dissolved, but expanded by others. People's hearts still needed preparation; and as long as hearts are in need of preparation, our task is not finished either.

John could only speak earthly truth to people.[9] His baptism could lead people to the King; but only the King, through the baptism of the Spirit, could transform people in their value systems and bring them into the Kingdom. For transformation to be complete, you must move beyond John's baptism (knowledge of who the King is) to Spirit baptism.

---

5. Matthew 3:11-12 "I baptize you with water for repentance, but he who is coming after me is mightier than I, whose sandals I am not worthy to carry. He will baptize you with the Holy Spirit and with fire. His winnowing fork is in his hand, and he will clear his threshing floor and gather his wheat into the barn, but the chaff he will burn with unquenchable fire."

6. John 1:29-34 The next day he saw Jesus coming toward him, and said, "Behold, the Lamb of God, who takes away the sin of the world! This is he of whom I said, 'After me comes a man who ranks before me, because he was before me.' I myself did not know him, but for this purpose I came baptizing with water, that he might be revealed to Israel." And John bore witness: "I saw the Spirit descend from heaven like a dove, and it remained on him. I myself did not know him, but he who sent me to baptize with water said to me, 'He on whom you see the Spirit descend and remain, this is he who baptizes with the Holy Spirit.' And I have seen and have borne witness that this is the Son of God."

7. John 3:5

8. John 4:2

9. John 3:31

John's misunderstanding

Near the end of his ministry while John was in prison, he sent some of his disciples to ask Jesus, "Are you the one who is to come, or shall we look for another?"[10] John, whose job it was to prepare the way for the Messiah, now asked Jesus if he was the only Messiah! It seems the prophet of God was shaken.

Jesus sent John's disciples back with instructions to tell John what he was doing: "The blind receive their sight and the lame walk, lepers are cleansed and the deaf hear, and the dead are raised up, and the poor have good news preached to them." Then he added, "And blessed is the one who is not offended by me." Jesus told John not to be offended by him!

Remember, John was the chief shovel man for the Messiah. However, he was in prison, and was totally demoralized by his situation. The Messianic Kingdom was not working out as he had imagined. If the King from God was here, John could not see why he should still be in prison.

John came fulfilling the prophecies made about Elijah, a great man written about in the Old Testament. Elijah had a confrontation with the priests of Baal that culminated with his calling down fire from heaven.[11] Then he, too, became demoralized because Jezebel, the queen of Israel, opposed him and threatened to kill him.[12] So, Elijah ran away. That illustrates the emotional state of John.

John taught that the Messiah was coming with a winnowing fork and would bring judgment and burn up the chaff. But John was not seeing any judgment. If Jesus truly was the Messiah, John was ready for a kingdom and a nice prison break![13] He was probably thinking, "Get on with it, Jesus! This would be a really good time to have your kingdom come."

Jesus quoted from Isaiah,[14] a book powerful in the ministries of

---

10. Matthew 11

11. 1 Kings 18

12. 1 Kings 19

13. Isaiah 61:1 The Spirit of the Lord God is upon me, because the Lord has anointed me to bring good news to the poor; he has sent me to bind up the brokenhearted, to proclaim liberty to the captives, and the opening of the prison to those who are bound…

14. Isaiah 35:5-6 Then the eyes of the blind shall be opened, and the ears of the deaf

both Jesus and John. The crucial Kingdom message was being preached and the blessings that were to come in the Messianic Kingdom were happening: miracles, healings, and the preaching of the good news to the poor.

In his response to John, Jesus never mentioned the judgment spoken of throughout the book of Isaiah.[15] He stopped short of it. Instead, Jesus listed all the blessings of the Kingdom and added one more to it: "Blessed is the one who does not fall away because of me."[16] Jesus sent John's disciples back with the message that the judgment was not happening now: it was postponed. How would you like to be John at that point? He probably thought, "I'm never getting out of here!"

As John's disciples went away, Jesus spoke to the crowd concerning John. John was a very important man and Jesus loved him very much. Jesus did not want anyone to have the wrong impression of John or to speak negatively about him. John was in prison and naturally felt depressed.

"What did you go out into the wilderness to see?" Jesus asked. Jesus wanted them to remember when John first came as the voice crying in the wilderness. He wanted them to remember the man in the desert wearing camel hair and eating locusts. *That man* was no reed shaken by the wind. He was a man who spoke powerfully from God. He spoke of the blessings of the Kingdom; he spoke of the judgment of God.

"Did you go to see someone dressed in soft clothing like a king in a palace who locked people in prison?" They went out to see a prophet and saw not only a prophet, but more than a prophet; for John had prepared the way for the King. Jesus then declared that no one born of women had been greater than John the Baptist. Now, if Jesus says that about you, it really means something.

Then Jesus taught that the least person in his Kingdom was greater than John. It does not matter how many miracles or healings or blessings there may be, you still must have faith that Jesus is the King.

---

unstopped; then shall the lame man leap like a deer, and the tongue of the mute sing for joy. For waters break forth in the wilderness, and streams in the desert…

15. Isaiah 35:4 Say to those who have an anxious heart, "Be strong; fear not! Behold, your God will come with vengeance, with the recompense of God. He will come and save you."

16. Matthew 11:6 And blessed is the one who is not offended by me.

When Jesus said, "Blessed is the one who is not offended by me," he was saying to John, "John, you must trust me. Do not look for a second Messiah. Do not look for another to follow. Do not look for one person who brings blessing and another who brings judgment. I am the one, but you must trust me. You must have faith in me." Even John needed faith. When John read the Old Testament he did not understand everything about the Kingdom, so he had to trust that Jesus did. The Old Testament prophesied the coming of the Messiah, but no one, not even John, fully understood it.

John the Baptist needed to be reminded that he did not have a shovel. Somewhere along the way, he forgot; or perhaps he thought maybe later there would be a shovel and an earthly kingdom. Instead, Jesus was saying to John, "There is no shovel." Our thinking about the Kingdom must come only from what Jesus said about the Kingdom, not from our possible misunderstandings of the Old Testament. Otherwise, we will become demoralized like John was in prison. We will stand around saying something like, "Where is the kingdom that he promised?"

John's problem was not instability or fickleness. His problem was that he did not understand the Old Testament. Even the greatest prophet of the Old Covenant, John the Baptist, did not grasp everything about the Kingdom. No Old Testament prophet understood the Kingdom perfectly; they saw at a distance. So Jesus defended John by reminding the people of whom they went out to see, and by reminding them of how excited they were when they thought God spoke to them again. Jesus reminded them of how their hearts were prepared by John and how they repented. Then Jesus stated that John was the Elijah who was to come.

Restoring hearts to the Father

Jesus took three of his disciples to the top of a mountain, and there before them, he was transfigured.[17] Jesus' glory was displayed and the disciples were stunned as they stood before his bright, shining form. While this was happening, Moses and Elijah appeared. These two men represented the Law and the Prophets from the Old Testament.

When they descended the mountain, Jesus told his disciples not to tell anyone what they had seen until he had been raised from the dead.

17. Matthew 17

The disciples then asked, "Why do the scribes say that first Elijah must come?" They were curious about this because, only moments before, Elijah had been standing before them, and because Jesus had already identified John the Baptist as the Elijah to come. John was the Elijah; but he was unrecognized and rejected, even as Jesus would be unrecognized and rejected.

The main point here is that the disciples were asking the same question that John the Baptist asked when he was in prison. To understand this, we must look at Malachi 4:4-6.

> *"Remember the law of my servant Moses, the statutes and rules that I commanded him at Horeb for all Israel. Behold, I will send you Elijah the prophet before the great and awesome day of the Lord comes. And he will turn the hearts of fathers to their children and the hearts of children to their fathers, lest I come and strike the land with a decree of utter destruction."*

This text is about Moses and Elijah, whom the disciples had previously witnessed. No wonder they asked Jesus about this passage. John knew he was the Elijah to come, and he was expecting the great and awesome day of the Lord. From this text we also see that John's role was to turn the hearts of the fathers to the children and the hearts of the children to their fathers.

Jesus had said, "Tell no one the vision, until the Son of Man is raised from the dead." Thus, the disciples were really asking Jesus about his dying. Their real question was: "If you are going to die, then did John (Elijah) really bring restoration?" Even as John had trouble with being in prison if Jesus was the Messianic King, so also the disciples did not understand the "success" of Elijah with John in prison and Jesus talking about dying. In other words, "If the Kingdom is coming, why is the Messiah going to die?" Jesus answered that Elijah (John) died doing his mission, and the Messiah would also die doing his mission. It was part of the plan of restoration.

The scribes understood the prophecies about the Messiah only partially, yet so did John the Baptist and the disciples. The scribes assumed they would recognize Elijah when he came. How could you miss someone like Elijah? But they missed him. They rejected John because he did not have a shovel! In rejecting John, they ultimately rejected the Messiah. They were looking for an earthly kingdom and could not get past that dream, which inevitably led them to the destruction of the land mentioned in Malachi 4:6.

John the Baptist's mission was to prepare the way for the Lord. Although he came to show the people who the King was, the least in the Kingdom does it better than he did because the least in the Kingdom more correctly identifies the King. The least in the Kingdom better understands that Jesus' Kingdom is not an earthly kingdom, but a spiritual Kingdom.

When they reached the bottom of the mountain, Jesus saw a crowd of people, and a man came and knelt before him. He begged Jesus to restore his ill son to him. Jesus' response to those present startles me. He said, "O faithless and twisted generation, how long am I to be with you? How long am I to bear with you?"

Jesus was not angry with the father; he was bothered that his disciples were unable to heal the boy, restoring him to his father. His disciples were failing at their mission. By now they were supposed to be able to turn the hearts of fathers to their children and the children to their fathers. That was the point of this living parable to which Jesus brought his disciples.

Isaiah 40 begins a large section in Isaiah about the coming Servant of the Lord, the Messiah. It commences with a voice crying in the wilderness, preparing the way for the King. This was the coming of Elijah, the role of John the Baptist. Three chapters later, we read of the very dangers being used to destroy the demon-possessed boy: fire and water.[18]

> *When you pass through the waters, I will be with you; and through the rivers, they shall not overwhelm you; when you walk through fire you shall not be burned, and the flame shall not consume you.*[19]

The scribes, the disciples, and Jesus would all know this Messianic passage. I do not believe it was a coincidence that the symptoms the boy faced were precisely those related to the deliverance passage in Isaiah. Neither do I think it was a coincidence that Jesus and his disciples were discussing this on their way down the mountain.

Isaiah 43:2 speaks of God the Father restoring his people back to

---

18. Matthew 11:14-15 And when they came to the crowd, a man came up to him and, kneeling before him, said, "Lord, have mercy on my son, for he is an epileptic and he suffers terribly. For often he falls into the fire, and often into the water."

19. Isaiah 43:2

himself. This teaches us that the disciples were expected to take up the role of John the Baptist. That was their new mission. They were the ones now called to make the way smooth in the hearts of men and women, preparing the way for Israel to be restored to the Father. It was now their job.

The least in the Kingdom points to the King. You had your heart prepared to come to the Father, and you know who the King is. But it cannot stop with that, lest you be like the disciples whom Jesus rebuked. The disciples asked why they could not cast the demon out. He answered them, "Because of your little faith. For truly, I say to you, if you have faith like a grain of mustard seed, you will say to this mountain, 'Move from here to there,' and it will move, and nothing will be impossible for you." Is Jesus talking about moving literal mountains? Of course not! He is talking about the mountains in the hearts of people that need to be removed for the coming of the King.

Each person in the Kingdom, even the least, has the job of telling people who the King is. All those in the Kingdom are to remove obstacles and prepare the hearts of others to receive the King. We do this through pointing out who the King is, by describing the Kingdom as spiritual and not earthly, and by living and teaching the value system of the Kingdom. If you do not do these, you will be rebuked for your little faith. However, when you do step out in faith and attempt to restore people to God the Father, Jesus said it would happen. You become the mover of mountains by faith. You take up the role of Elijah and of John the Baptist by faith.

The Great Commission

There is one more place we must look before we are finished with John the Baptist. Although he is not mentioned in this text, the role that we have been assigned is mentioned. In the passage known as the Great Commission, we are given the job of baptism.

> *And Jesus came and said to them, "All authority in heaven and on earth has been given to me. Go therefore and make disciples of all nations, baptizing them in the name of the Father and of the Son and of the Holy Spirit, teaching them to observe all that I have commanded you. And behold, I am with you always, to the end of the age."*[20]

20. Matthew 28:18-20

Once Jesus was resurrected from the dead, he spoke of the full establishment of his Kingdom: "All authority in heaven and on earth has been given to me." Out of this came Jesus' command to his disciples to go and make more disciples. What interests me most is the specific way in which he spoke of our fulfilling that command.

Jesus taught that disciples are made through baptizing and teaching. It should be clear to us now what this entails. Baptizing is the process by which people's hearts are prepared for the King.

Water baptism is only one part of the work of John. His more important work was his calling people to repentance, along with his identification of Jesus Christ as King. If we narrow baptism to only water baptism,[21] we lose the significance of John's work *as a whole*. We also delay baptizing disciples far beyond the example set in the New Testament. Water baptism was practiced as part of the evangelistic message, and not delayed until confidence in a person's knowledge or faithfulness could be established.

Once people's hearts are prepared for the King, they can enter the Kingdom. And what do we teach them about coming into the Kingdom? That they must observe everything Jesus has commanded. In other words, they must adopt the value system of the King and the Kingdom. They must have sacrificial love for the benefit of others.

People first receive John's baptism, which is an acceptance of the identity of the King. In the New Testament, water baptism accompanied this preparation. However, that is only a start; it does not provide life. Your heart may be prepared for the King, but you still must receive the King. This explains why so many could hear Jesus teach, but still not be saved at the end of the day. They wanted a king, but not one who called them to sacrificial love as he did. What the King demands is costly and requires deep transformation.

21. Baptism in the New Testament has additional nuances that vary according to context.

B Justification, Sanctification, and Glorification

When teaching the doctrine of justification, I previously have used a legal approach in explaining our sin and Christ's righteousness. Our sin is a debt we owe to God, which he forgives by accepting the death of Christ as payment for our sin. Legally our sin is transferred to Christ, and his righteousness is transferred to us.

Paul explained justification in legal terms because he was dealing with the transition from Law[1] to grace. He spoke of our moving from the realm of death to the realm of life by our death to the Law, along with Christ on the cross. We cannot go on living under Law because we cannot enter the Kingdom of God through the Law. Those under the Mosaic Covenant must die to it and enter the New Covenant.

Paul also wrote that the purpose of the Law was to increase transgression.[2] As God gave commandments, it became clear to men that they could not keep them. This highlighted the differences between God's values and man's. Although the Law only partially revealed God's value system, man was still unable to do it. Thus, the Law increased man's sense of need for God's grace.

Paul also wrote that we are under the dominion of sin. Sin and death were both present before the Law, as evidenced by men dying

1. By "Law" I refer to the Law of Moses, or the Mosaic Law.
2. Romans 5:20

from Adam to Moses, even though they broke no specific laws from God.[3] Paul then asked the question, "How are we released from the Law?"[4] There are two main interpretations of his answer.

The first interpretation views Paul writing as a Jew under the Law. Once he saw God's value system as declared in the Law, he began to realize how unlike God he really was. Even those under the Law who saw the glory of God in it and desired to practice it failed at doing it. The second interpretation views Paul writing as a Christian who still fails at living God's value system, but that failure is not debilitating and will eventually be undone. Either way, sin reigns in the realm of death because death is the place where people are not doing God's value system, but rather their own. It is the place of death because they are out of relationship with God.

Jesus came to redeem those under the Law. Redemption has to do with slavery; a slavery that is not only to the Law, but also to sin in the realm of death. We know this because Christ came not only to those under the Law (Jews), but also to those without the Law (Gentiles).

Do not miss the significance of that last point. I am a Gentile born in the twentieth century. I never lived *one day* under the Law. However, I was still in the realm of sin and death. Any interpretation of justification must go beyond the Law in explaining God's dealings with Gentiles.

Understanding sin in terms of relationship

Now when I teach the doctrine of justification, instead of using a legal approach, I examine the work of Christ in terms of relationship and value system. First, sin and righteousness must be understood in terms of value system.

Imagine two partially overlapping circles. One circle represents God's value system and the other your own. God is perfect, so everything in his value system is good. It is the true measure of holiness. The parts of your circle that do not overlap with God's are sin. Sin is your rebellion against God's value system. It is your failing at the three areas of temptation (bodily appetites, prestige, and worldly kingdom).[5] You cannot have relationship with God if even *one* of your values is

3. Romans 5:12-14
4. Romans 7
5. Matthew 4

different. This includes not only the values you act on, but also the ones you hold in your heart. That is why you can never gain salvation, which is relationship with God, on your own.

We all sin even though we do not all break the Law. We did not break the commandment given to Adam,[6] and we are not all Jews born under the Law. Nevertheless, we all die because we continue to live our own value systems that are unlike God's.[7] We are born into a cursed world, to cursed parents, and we inherit the curse and live it ourselves.

Relationship with God is based on having *exactly* the same value system as his. He is perfect and will not have relationship with you if you do not share his perfect holiness.[8] Jesus and the Father have perfect relationship because they perfectly share the same value system. We do not share that relationship with them because we do not perfectly share their value system. This is why we are condemned and live in the realm of sin and death, out of relationship with God.

Salvation is a restoration of relationship

Never forget that Jesus' death on the cross was about relationship. Death is a relational term. When Jesus died on the cross, he was rejected by both man and God.

When men crucified Jesus, it revealed how different their value systems were from his. Jesus called people to a value system of love, yet they rejected it and murdered him. This revelation of man's value system continues today with all those who reject him. The Gospel must be presented in terms of value system so people can see that rejection of Christ is also a rejection of the value system of the Kingdom.

On the cross, Jesus was rejected by his Father. This is the important part for us theologically in salvation. When Jesus died on the cross, the Father turned his face away from him. If God shines his face on you, you are blessed; if he turns his back toward you, you are

6. Genesis 2:16-17 And the Lord God commanded the man, saying, "You may surely eat of every tree of the garden, but of the tree of the knowledge of good and evil you shall not eat, for in the day that you eat of it you shall surely die."

7. Romans 5:12-14 Therefore, just as sin came into the world through one man, and death through sin, and so death spread to all men because all sinned—for sin indeed was in the world before the law was given, but sin is not counted where there is no law. Yet death reigned from Adam to Moses, even over those whose sinning was not like the transgression of Adam, who was a type of the one who was to come.

8. Holiness is being completely separate from anything not in God's value system.

cursed.[9] Jesus was cursed on the cross for our rebellion against the value system of God. He experienced death—loss of relationship with the Father—on our behalf. Jesus died for our rebellion: he died for the parts of our value systems that are not like God's.

Christ's death is a propitiation for our sins. In other words, he died to remove God's wrath against us. Sin must *always* be dealt with. Forgiveness is not pretending that something never happened. The forgiver acknowledges the reality of the offense and makes payment for it himself.

Jesus died for the sin that put us in the place of death. Death is being out of relationship with God. Now we can see the full beauty of the resurrection. On the cross, Jesus took on the loss of relationship that was due us. Yet he could not remain out of relationship with the Father because *his* value system was still perfectly like the Father's. Jesus rose bodily from the dead to demonstrate his power over death, both spiritual and physical. In other words, his resurrection is all about relationship!

Christ's resurrection powerfully shows the triumph of his value system over the value systems of men. They rejected him and crucified him, but his value system of sacrificial love used the ugliness of their value systems to show how ugly they really were. The sinful values that crucified Christ allowed him to fully demonstrate his own value of sacrificial love for the benefit of others. Those who crucified Christ did not understand that it was really a battle of value systems at the cross. If they had known this, they never would have crucified Christ.[10] This, again, is why evangelism must focus on value system.

The King Representative

Jesus experienced broken relationship with the Father so that our relationship could be restored. Even though the penalty for our value systems has been paid, God still cannot have relationship with us. He cannot pretend that we share his value system when, in fact, we still do not.

9. Numbers 6:22-27 The Lord spoke to Moses, saying, "Speak to Aaron and his sons, saying, Thus you shall bless the people of Israel: you shall say to them, The Lord bless you and keep you; the Lord make his face to shine upon you and be gracious to you; the Lord lift up his countenance upon you and give you peace. So shall they put my name upon the people of Israel, and I will bless them."

10. 1 Corinthians 2:8 None of the rulers of this age understood this, for if they had, they would not have crucified the Lord of glory.

With the advent of the Davidic Covenant, of which Jesus Christ is the fulfillment, there came a significant change for the nation of Israel. Prior to this, God dealt with the people as a community. Under Joshua, even one man's sin could endanger the whole community.[11] During the time of the Judges, God disciplined whole communities in order to turn them back to him.

In the Davidic Covenant, God promised to give David's son an everlasting kingdom.[12] However, the conditional part of the Covenant required that the son must share the value system of his father David. The big shift at this time was that the king became the representative of the people before God. No longer was each person in Israel affecting how God treated the community. The transition from individual under Joshua, to warrior under the Judges, now moved to the king under David.

Even with this shift to the king representative, the question still remained: "Is God the King?" God was the King of the entire community; the kings who understood it were blessed, and those who rejected it were cursed. David understood this, and Isaiah experienced it firsthand in the temple with his vision of God as King.[13] God wanted people to be like David, adopting his value system. After David, each king in Judea was measured by this one standard: Did they have a heart for God like David?

Under the Davidic Covenant, God began dealing with the nation based on the value system of their king. If the king obeyed God, the people were blessed. If the king was evil, the people came under God's judgment. When the people of Judea were expelled from their land, it was ultimately because of their kings. This was partially because "as goes the king, so goes the kingdom." But we must not fail to see the reason for final judgment. God considered the actions of Manasseh as the reason for the captivity.[14] Even the godly King Josiah could not

---

11. Joshua 7

12. 2 Samuel 7

13. Isaiah 6

14. 2 Kings 21:10-15 And the Lord said by his servants the prophets, "Because Manasseh king of Judah has committed these abominations and has done things more evil than all that the Amorites did, who were before him, and has made Judah also to sin with his idols, therefore thus says the Lord, the God of Israel: Behold, I am bringing upon Jerusalem and Judah such disaster that the ears of everyone who hears of it will tingle. And I will stretch over Jerusalem the measuring line of Samaria, and the plumb line of the house of Ahab, and I will wipe Jerusalem as one wipes a dish, wiping

undo the promised judgment for the sin of Manasseh.[15]

When we come into Christ's Kingdom, Jesus becomes our King Representative before God. This is very important. Remember, righteousness is *doing* God's value system. Holiness is being separate from the value systems of the world. Christ is righteous because he perfectly does God's value system, and he is holy because he has no rebellion against God in him. Once we enter Christ's Kingdom, Jesus stands before God as our King Representative. God treats us not according to our own value systems, but according to the value system of our King. Christ died for all those in his Kingdom, and he represents them all before God under the New Covenant.

Sanctification

The New Testament teaches two kinds of sanctification. First, there is our positional sanctification. That is our status "in Christ," our place under our King Representative. This allows God to have relationship with us in this life *even though* we do not fully share his value system.

This is not an issue of his love for us; it is an issue of having relationship with us. God's love sacrificed his Son on the cross, so we know that he is not forced into loving us against his will. He loved us while we were still his enemies, but he cannot have relationship with us while we continue to rebel against him. Therefore, our relationship with God, in this life, is based on Jesus being our King.

The second kind of sanctification is our progressive or practical sanctification. This is our adoption of God's value system as our own during this life. We put off our old value systems and put on a new one in Christ. For this difficult task, we require the powerful help of the Holy Spirit.

---

it and turning it upside down. And I will forsake the remnant of my heritage and give them into the hand of their enemies, and they shall become a prey and a spoil to all their enemies, because they have done what is evil in my sight and have provoked me to anger, since the day their fathers came out of Egypt, even to this day."

15. 2 Kings 23:25-27 Before him there was no king like him, who turned to the Lord with all his heart and with all his soul and with all his might, according to all the Law of Moses, nor did any like him arise after him. Still the Lord did not turn from the burning of his great wrath, by which his anger was kindled against Judah, because of all the provocations with which Manasseh had provoked him. And the Lord said, "I will remove Judah also out of my sight, as I have removed Israel, and I will cast off this city that I have chosen, Jerusalem, and the house of which I said, My name shall be there."

For us to be practically sanctified, the Holy Spirit must first indwell us; but he cannot fellowship with those whose value systems are not like his. Our problem is circular: we cannot be made holy by the Spirit because we are not holy enough to have him indwell us in order to make us holy. This explains why Christ first needed to ascend to his place as King of the Kingdom of God in heaven prior to the coming of the Holy Spirit. The Holy Spirit could not indwell us (have relationship with us) until Christ fully took up his position as King Representative on our behalf.

Once we enter into relationship with God based on his status as our King, God's Spirit can indwell us and transform us into his likeness. The progressive change in our values is variously spoken of by Paul as putting off the old man,[16] being crucified with Christ,[17] crucifying the flesh,[18] and being crucified to the world.[19]

Glorification

Transformation by sanctification in this life is part of our glorification.[20] The glory we have in this life is demonstrated by how much our value systems are transformed into the value system of God. One day we will be fully glorified.[21] In other words, our value systems will be exactly like God's, without any rebellion in them. Of course, that will not happen until we arrive in heaven.

In heaven, we will no longer need relationship with the Father

---

16. Ephesians 4:20-24 But that is not the way you learned Christ!—assuming that you have heard about him and were taught in him, as the truth is in Jesus, to put off your old self, which belongs to your former manner of life and is corrupt through deceitful desires, and to be renewed in the spirit of your minds, and to put on the new self, created after the likeness of God in true righteousness and holiness.

Colossians 3:9-10 Do not lie to one another, seeing that you have put off the old self with its practices and have put on the new self, which is being renewed in knowledge after the image of its creator.

17. Galatians 2:19 For through the law I died to the law, so that I might live to God. I have been crucified with Christ.

18. Galatians 5:24 And those who belong to Christ Jesus have crucified the flesh with its passions and desires.

19. Galatians 6:14 But far be it from me to boast except in the cross of our Lord Jesus Christ, by which the world has been crucified to me, and I to the world.

20. See Chapter 6: The Law Cannot Transform

21. Romans 8:16-17 The Spirit himself bears witness with our spirit that we are children of God, and if children, then heirs—heirs of God and fellow heirs with Christ, provided we suffer with him in order that we may also be glorified with him.

based on the value system of our King Representative. We will be able to enter into relationship with him on our own. In heaven, we will be perfectly righteous and perfectly holy. In other words, we will perfectly have and perfectly do God's value system. The rebellious nature of the Fall will be completely undone, and we will not value anything different from him. In heaven, we will perfectly share God's value system.

C Jesus' Finances

We often assume that Jesus was very poor. This assumption can lead us to misinterpret some New Testament passages. Although Jesus himself may not have possessed much, it does not follow that he and his disciples did not have more significant shared resources. Let me give a few reasons why I believe Jesus and his entourage were not poor.

First, we must understand the distinction between being rich and having a regular supply of funds or some savings. When someone was mentioned as rich, they possessed wealth far in excess of their needs. Having savings, even as much as several months' worth, does not constitute being rich.

For example, a woman anointed Jesus with an expensive ointment or perfume.[1] Although this perfume was very costly, owning it did not necessarily make the woman rich. If one woman could possess that much wealth, it is not difficult to believe Jesus' entire band could not possess a similar amount.

Second, Jesus was a teacher and healer. We know he was supported financially,[2] but he also would have received gifts from those whose lives he touched. When Jesus sent his disciples out to minister, he instructed them to receive their support from those they helped, although they could not demand payment for their services.[3]

---

1. Matthew 26:6-13
2. Luke 8:1-3
3. Matthew 10:5-10

Third, Jesus and his disciples constituted a group of thirteen men, aside from the additional people who travelled with them. At least some of those men could have drawn on private wealth. Matthew was a tax collector, and Peter, James and John owned their own fishing boat. They were not mere day-laborers or beggars. If each man brought enough to support himself for several weeks, the sum of their finances could have been quite large.

Fourth, Judas was known to have skimmed from the money bag.[4] If the coins contained were extremely limited, he would have been very bold to attempt stealing from the group since it would have been so obvious.

Finally, I must also address the temple tax.[5] There is no reason to believe that Jesus and Peter were unable to pay it. The miraculous nature of the provision, as explained by Jesus, was an issue of whether or not they needed to pay it at all. Jesus paid it only not to offend; but in essence, he did not pay it himself.

4. John 12:6

5. Matthew 17:24-27

D Glossary of Theological Terms

Baptism – Acknowledgement of a heart's preparation to receive Jesus as King.

Confession – Agreeing with God that you do not share his value system, and with his assessment that yours deserves condemnation.

Death – Being out of relationship with God because of a difference in value system. Physical death becomes like sleep for the Christian because relationship is not permanently interrupted. Eternal death is eternally and permanently being out of relationship with God.

Faith – Believing the promises of God.

Forgiveness – As sinner, not being punished for the consequences of your sinful value system. As forgiver, choosing not to allow a person's *previous* value system to stand in the way of the *current* relationship.

Glorification – The adoption of God's value system as our own.

God's value system – Sacrificial love for the benefit of others. It most looks like Jesus Christ dying on the cross.

Grace – Receiving the blessing of relationship even though you deserve cursing because of your value system.

Holiness – Being separate from the value systems of the world.

Humility – An accurate assessment of your value system as compared to God's.

Idolatry – Giving precedence to anything you value more than God.

Life – Being in relationship with God. Eternal life describes not only duration but quality of relationship.

Propitiation – The removal of wrath resulting in a state of relational peace.

Reconciliation – Restoration of relationship based on an agreement of value system.

Repentance – Adopting God's value system and rejecting your own.

Righteousness – Doing God's value system.

Saint – A person within the Kingdom of God who has Jesus Christ as his King Representative.

Sanctification, positional – Our place in relationship with God based on Jesus Christ, our King Representative.

Sanctification, practical – The process by which we adopt God's value system as our own.

Sin – Any value held in the heart that does not conform to the value system of God.

Acknowledgements

As a pastor, my thinking has been influenced by the many books I have read and studied, as well as by the speakers and teachers I have had the benefit of hearing throughout the course of my life. Regrettably, I am unable to list all the sources that have shaped my thoughts over the years. However, I am thankful for all those who have gone before me and who have helped shape my faith.

I thank my congregation for the opportunity to serve them as their pastor and teacher. Without the time and encouragement to study, this book would never have been possible.

I thank my wife, Melissa, for proofreading and giving suggestions on how to better express my thoughts, as well as for her encouragement during the long writing process.

I thank those who read and gave feedback during the creation of this manuscript: Wayne Jacobson, Larry Grove and Breck Haining. Special thanks to Valerie Casper for editing and proofreading this work.

Finally, I would like to thank you, my reader. As a pastor, I am more comfortable speaking my thoughts than writing them, and I am aware that this book fails to adequately express my ideas in clear and concise language.

Selected Bibliography

Carson, D. A. *The Expositor's Bible Commentary.* Vol. 8, *Matthew, Mark, Luke.* Edited by Frank E. Gaebelein. Grand Rapids: Zondervan, 1984.

Moo, Douglas J. *The Epistle to the Romans.* Grand Rapids: Eerdmans, 1996.

Morris, Leon. *The Gospel According to John.* Grand Rapids: Eerdmans, 1971.

Patterson, R. D., and Austel, Hermann J. *The Expositor's Bible Commentary.* Vol. 4. Edited by Frank E. Gaebelein. Grand Rapids: Zondervan, 1988.

Printed in the United States
215484BV00006B/2/P

9 780982 357408